Armies of the American Revolution, 1775-1783

Part 1: George Washington's military forces

By
Gabriele Esposito

Color plates by

Benedetto Esposito

Armies of the American Revolution, 1775-1783:Part 1: George Washington's Military Forces
By Gabriele Esposito
Cover by Hugh Charles McBarron, Jr (Department of the Army)
Illustrations by Benedetto Esposito
This edition published in 2021

Winged Hussar Publishing, is an imprint of Winged Hussar Publishing, LLC
1525 Hulse Rd, Unit 1, Point Pleasant, NJ 08742
Copyright © Winged Hussar Publishing, LLC
ISBN 978-1-950423-60-6
LCN 2021939566

Bibliographical References and Index
1. History. 2. United States. 3. American Revolution

Winged Hussar Publishing, LLC All rights reserved
For more information on Winged Hussar Publishing, LLC,
Visit us at www.whpsupplyroom.com & www.wingedhussarpublishing.com

This book is sold subject to the condition that it shall not, by way of trade or otherwise, be lent, resold, hired out, or otherwise circulated without the publisher's prior consent in any form of binding or cover other than that in which it is published and without a similar condition, including this condition, being imposed on the subsequent purchaser.

The scanning, uploading, and distribution of this book via the Internet or via any other means without the permission of the publisher is illegal and punishable by law. Please purchase only authorized electronic editions, and do not participate in or encourage electronic piracy of copyrighted materials. Your support of the author's and publisher's rights is appreciated. Karma, it's everywhere

Preface

The main aim of this book is to present a detailed overview of the organization and uniforms of the American military forces that fought during the Revolution of 1775-1783. The creation of the present work would have been impossible without the fundamental support of Vincent Rospond, editor of Winged Hussar Publishing, who enjoyed the idea behind this project since the beginning. The magnificent eight colour plates illustrating this book have been realized by the "maestro" Benedetto Esposito, whose artistic capabilities and vivid style have brought George Washington's soldiers to life again after two centuries. His collaboration has been a splendid one, as can be expected by a son from his father. This book is dedicated to him and to my mother, Maria Rosaria Grassito. A very special thanks goes to Olivier Millet, a great researcher and friend, for giving me permission to use the fantastic uniform plates that he has created on the Continental Army. Olivier Millet has a fantastic blog which displays most of his personal researches and colour plates: http://history-uniforms.over-blog.com/. Finally, I want to express all my deep gratitude for the two groups of reenactors that provided the magnificent photos illustrating the present work: the *2nd South Carolina Regiment of the Continental Line* and the *1st Virginia Regiment of the Continental Line*. The collaboration of Erick Nason, from the former group, was absolutely fundamental for my research.

Chronology

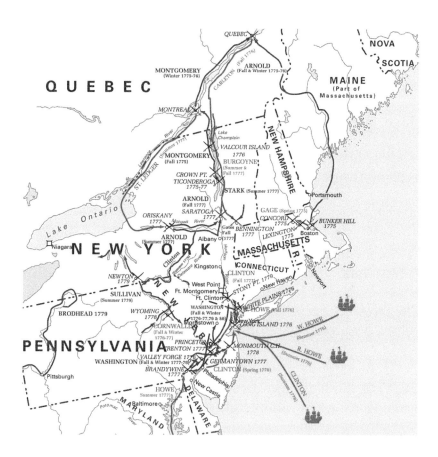

- **1765 – 1772:** In the wake of the French-Indian War, the English Parliament imposes a series of taxes on the Thirteen Colonies; these are opposed by a portion of the American population in a series of assemblies.

- **February 1775**: Massachusetts is declared in a state of rebellion; the British military forces in the Boston area receive orders to disarm the local militiamen and arrest their leaders.

- **April 19, 1775**: the Battles of Lexington and Concord take place in Middlesex County, Massachusetts. In the first engagements of the American Revolution the British troops are able to destroy supplies that had been stored by the rebels but are attacked during their retreat to Boston. The patriot "minutemen" cause heavy losses to the enemy without suffering significant casualties. After these events, royal officials are expelled from the Thirteen Colonies and Boston comes under siege from the militias of New England.

- **June 14, 1775**: the Continental Army, is organized under command of George Washington,.

- **June 17, 1775**: Battle of Bunker Hill (Charlestown, Massachusetts). The British military forces capture the Charlestown Peninsula after suffering heavy losses but are unable to break the siege of Boston. Following this clash, the Americans launch an invasion of Canada with the objective of conquering Quebec.

- **August 23, 1775**: King George III issues a "Proclamation of Rebellion", according to which the Second Continental Congress (organized by the Thirteen Colonies in May) is declared illegal.

- **March 17, 1776**: the Continental Army forces the British garrison to evacuate Boston.

- **June 29, 1776**: the first elements of a large British expeditionary force arrive in New York Bay. By the end of August, some 32,000 British troops are camped on Staten Island.

- **July 4, 1776**: United States Declaration of Independence.

- **August 27, 1776**: the Continental Army is defeated by the British military forces at the Battle of Brooklyn. New York City and Long Island are occupied by the British Army.

- **October 1776**: the American invasion of Canada ends in complete failure, with a cost of over 10,000 casualties. Meanwhile the British Army gradually occupies New Jersey moving from New York.

- **December 25, 1776**: Washington crosses the Delaware River at the head of his army, with the objective of reconquering New Jersey from the British.

- **December 26, 1776**: Battle of Trenton, the first victory of the Continental Army in New Jersey.

- **January 3, 1777**: Battle of Princeton, the defeated British troops are obliged to evacuate New Jersey.

- **June 14, 1777**: a British military force with 7,000 soldiers moves from Canada with the objective of joining the British troops in New York and of isolating New England from the rest of the Thirteen Colonies.

- **August 1777**: the British Army in New York, instead of joining forces with the troops coming from Canada, lands in Pennsylvania.

- **September 19, 1777**: the British invasion force advancing from Canada is defeated at the First Battle of Saratoga.

- **September 26, 1777**: the British troops in Pennsylvania capture Philadelphia but are unable to obtain further gains in this theatre of operations.

- **October 7, 1777**: the British Army moving from Canada is decisively defeated at the Second Battle of Saratoga and is forced to surrender. This victory, the greatest for the Americans until that moment, convinces France to recognize the independence of the USA (February 6, 1778) and to begin hostilities with Great Britain (March 17, 1778).

- **November 15, 1777**: the first Constitution of the United States, the "Articles of Confederation and Perpetual Union", is promulgated.

- **December 1777 – May 1778**: at Valley Forge, Pennsylvania, George Washington reorganizes his Continental Army in view of the decisive phase of the American Revolution.

- **June 28, 1778**: the British troops evacuating Philadelphia are intercepted and defeated by the Continental Army at the Battle of Monmouth Court House. After this clash, the war in the northern territories becomes a stalemate, with the remaining British troops being blocked inside New York.

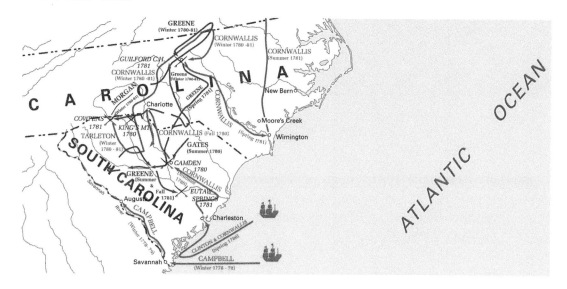

- **December 29, 1778**: a new British expeditionary force occupies Savannah, in Georgia.

- **May 12, 1780**: the British Army conquers Charleston, in South Carolina.

- **August 16, 1780**: the US military forces are defeated by the British at the Battle of Camden, in Kershaw County (South Carolina). After this victory, the British are in control of South

Carolina and Georgia.

- **October 7, 1780**: the Loyalists supporting the British in South Carolina are defeated at the Battle of Kings Mountain.

- **January 17, 1781**: the British Army is defeated at the Battle of Cowpens in South Carolina.

- **March 15, 1781**: after invading North Carolina, the British Army obtains an indecisive victory at the Battle of Guilford Court House.

- **May 20, 1781**: the British Army reaches Petersburg after moving into Virginia. During the following weeks the arrival of the Continental Army and of the French Army obliges the British to entrench themselves into a strong defensive position at Yorktown.

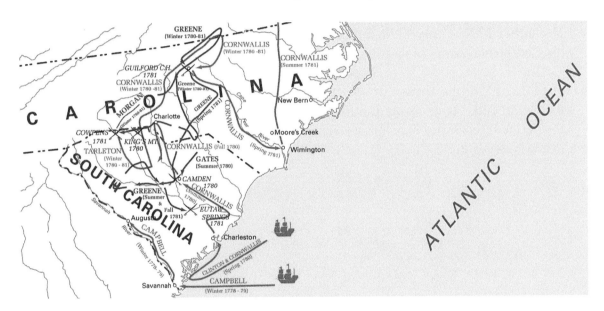

- **September – October 1781**: Siege of Yorktown, Virginia. The Americans, after having reconquered the last British strongholds in South Carolina and Georgia, besiege the British Army in Yorktown with the decisive support of the French Navy. The siege ends on 19 October, with the surrender of the defenders.

- **April 1782**: beginning of the peace negotiations between the USA and Great Britain. After the fall of Yorktown, no significant military operations took place in North America.

- **September 3, 1783**: the signing of the Treaty of Paris brings the hostilities to an end. Great Britain recognizes the independence of her former colonies.

- **November 25, 1783**: the last British troops abandon New York. End of the American Revolution.

The US Declaration of Independence, by John Trumbull.

The Military Situation of the Thirteen Colonies Before 1775

Since the early decades of colonization, the English settlers who migrated to the New World with their families organized some form of military units having a distinct "militia" character. At the beginning of the 17th century, England was one of the few European countries to have an effective general militia; the latter had been completely reorganized after 1588, when the menace represented by a Spanish invasion forced the English military authorities to create a new "auxiliary" organization that could support the regular army in case of foreign attack. The new English militia emerging from this reorganization was formed according to the "trained bands" system: the latter described how each able-bodied man of a community had to be available for military service in case of need and that he was obliged to undergo some compulsory military training during the course of each year.

All the militiamen of a community were assembled into a "trained band" and usually had to train at least once or twice in a year. The "trained bands" were not proper military units, but administrative ones that grouped all the individuals who were available for militia service (some social categories or some groups of workers, in fact, were exempt from the latter as part of their privileges). Generally speaking, when needed, the militiamen who made up a "trained band" were assembled into companies; each community, even the smallest village, could deploy at least one militia company (which numerical consistency could vary a lot). With the progression of time, especially during the bloody years of the English Civil War, the system of the "trained bands" became increasingly professional and the training sessions that had to be undergone by all militiamen became much more frequent. At the same time, the single companies started to be assembled into larger combat units that were defined as regiments. These were usually created by uniting all the militia companies coming from the same county together. Sometimes these county regiments could be very large and effective combat corps, especially in case of emergency. The single companies started to train once a week, usually on Sunday; the new county regiments, instead, usually trained only on some specific days of the year (when all the local militia companies were mustered). The English colonists who went to North America organized their militias exactly like those of their motherland; initially these were quite small and badly equipped, but with the progression of time and with the growing of colonial population they started to be an military resource. County regiments also began to be formed in the American colonies and some small units of cavalry and artillery were added to the usual infantry companies, thought they required more resources. The training of militia officers became more professional and serious, while tactics started to be modified in order to face the specific military needs of North America's woodlands. A real turning point in the history of the American militias was marked by the outbreak of King Philip's War in 1675: the latter was the greatest military emergency ever faced by the English colonists in the New World, since it saw the formation of a large native coalition that attacked the colonies of New England under command of the great warrior chief

Metacomet.

Initially the colonist's tactics did not work well in contrasting the rapid incursions of the native warriors, who used hit-and-run tactics based on guerrilla methods. The natives fought as raiders and were masters in organizing deadly ambushes; they had no idea of what "conventional warfare" was. As a result, the colonial militias could not fight against them by using the usual European tactics based on close formations and rigid discipline. In order to be effective, the American militiaman had to be an independent and flexible fighter who could be ready to move in less than a minute (hence the term "minuteman"). In addition, he had to be lightly equipped in order to travel long distances (mostly on foot) very rapidly also when moving on the broken terrain that covered most of North America (which comprised dense forests as well as unhealthy marshes). During King Philip's War, under guidance of the great tactician Benjamin Church, a first unit of such "new" militiamen was organized. Its members became known as "rangers" since their main task was that of patrolling the territory in order to intercept native raiders. After their success in King Philip's War, the rangers became an important component of the American militias. They ceased to be temporary corps and started to be made up of semi-professional "full-time" soldiers.

These rangers conducted reconnaissance missions on foot and horseback and garrisoned the main colonial fortifications that were built on the frontier with native territories. The rangers were able to repulse smaller enemy raids and were tasked with warning the rest of the militia when a larger native attack was launched. When the colonial military forces organized offensives directed against the natives, they were to provide scouts to the normal militia units. The first ranger company created by Benjamin Church in 1675 was trained by native warriors who were allies of the colonists; as a result, from their inception, ranger units learned how to fight with the same tactics of their direct opponents and as fast-moving light infantrymen. They were the "elite" of the colonial military apparatus and could fight in every condition. They could act as "special forces" to conduct raids or incursions but also as "mounted infantry", since they were trained to move as cavalrymen and to fight as infantrymen. The broken terrain of North America was not suitable for traditional cavalry tactics and thus mounted units could not be employed in a conventional way. Horses could be used to increase the mobility of the fighters, but not to conduct frontal charges: as a result, since the first decades of the 18th century, the few cavalry units deployed in North America started to act as mounted light infantrymen. The American militias of the colonial period were extremely "democratic" institutions, since the lower grade officers of each unit were usually elected by their own men (the higher grade officers one were appointed by the colonial authorities). Serving in the militia as an officer was an important component of a colonial politician's career and thus the military life of the early American communities was strongly linked to politics.

Until the outbreak of the French-Indian War in 1754, the British military presence in the American territories was sparse from a numerical point of view: at the beginning of the 18th century, for example, there were only four independent companies of infantry stationed in New York (whose members were all recruited from the local community and did not come from England). The scarce presence of British regulars in the American colonies was the result of several different factors. First of all, the English (and later British) government had never considered the American territories as important overseas territories; during the 18th century, for example, India was of much greater importance than the American colonies from an economic point of view and thus the British had no interest in spending large sums of money to garrison North America. In addition, it is important to bear in mind that most of the American colonies had a "difficult" relationship with the motherland. Those of New England, Massachusetts in particular, had been created by Puritan communities who had abandoned "Old England" in order to live according to their religious beliefs. In their motherland they were persecuted by the Church of England as "dissenters" and were treated as potentially dangerous religious extremists. In order to follow the "moral laws" contained in the Holy Bible and to avoid persecutions, thousands of Puritans migrated to North America during the 17th century. In their new homeland they lived in a very independent way, by practicing commerce and agriculture with excellent results; they began to feel removed from the Crown and thus had no intention to pay heavy taxes or to accept the presence of royal garrisons on their territories. During the English Civil War the colonies of New England supported the Parliamentarian cause and later sustained Cromwell's Commonwealth; as a result, when monarchy was restored in England during 1660, they found themselves in a difficult political position. During the following decades they resisted against all the attempts made by the monarchy to obtain a direct control over the political and economic activities of their new homeland. These included projects to increase the religious influence of the Church of England over the North American colonies as well as plans to send some garrisons to the American territories. In 1686, in order to exert a larger influence over the territories of North America, the English monarch James II ordered the "unification" of the four New England colonies (Massachusetts, Connecticut, Rhode Island and New Hampshire) into a "Dominion of New England". The latter, however, was very short-lived: when James II was replaced as King of England by William of Orange during the Glorious Revolution of 1688, in fact, the New Englanders rebelled against their pro-James governor and arrested him. These events, known as the "Boston Revolt of 1689", were just a preview of the future American Revolution. After them, it became clear in London that the colonies of New England had no intention to accept a strict control exerted by the motherland.

This was the political situation in New England at the beginning of the 18th century; in the other colonial territories of North America, however, the opinion that the settlers had of the motherland was different. In Virginia, Maryland and in the Carolinas the first colonial communities had not been created by religious dissenters like in New England but by settlers who were loyal to the Crown and who contained a high percentage of Catholics. As a result, especially in Virginia that had been the first "royal colony" of North America, the English political control was much more sensible than in the New England territories. In 1676, however, something started to change in Virginia due to the outbreak of a popular revolt that is commonly known as "Bacon's Rebellion". The latter saw the clash between the Virginia militia and the royal governor of the colony; it ended only after several massacres and after the arrival of an English regular regiment that was tasked with restoring order. In Virginia the local colonists also started to develop some sense of "national" identity and began considering themselves as "something different" from their motherland. As a result of the above, the year 1676 can be considered as a real turning point in American history: in New England, it was the victory of the northern colonies against the natives during King Philip's War; in Virginia, it saw the first major "American" rebellion against England. All this exactly one century before the outbreak of the American Revolution.

During the 17th century, while the English colonies flourished on the Atlantic coast, the French colonized Canada (at that time known as "New France") and established themselves very firmly on the North American soil. In contract to the English settlers, who were in search of new lands on which to expand their agricultural activities, the French settlers of Canada were more interested in obtaining control over the local fur trade. At that time, in fact, in Europe there was an increasing demand for the excellent furs coming from the woodlands of North America and thus fur commerce was an extremely lucrative economic activity. To obtain the best furs from the natives, the French had to establish peaceful relations with the latter; this was not something extremely difficult for them, also because they did not deprive the native communities of their lands as the English colonists did in the south. As a result of the above, New France soon started to flourish commercially. Despite

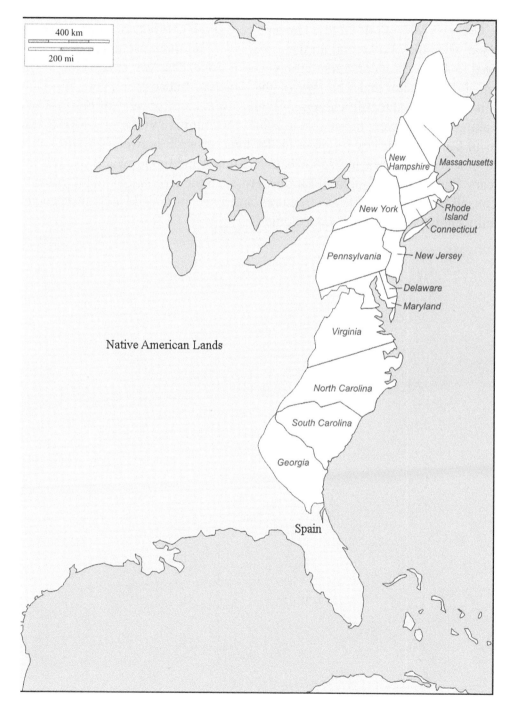

having a small population, it was quite strong from a military point of view thanks to the treaties of alliance that were signed by its authorities with the various native tribes living in Canada. By the end of 17th century, New France was ready to expand south and to menace the territorial integrity of northern New England. To face this new threat, the English colonists had no choice but to improve their militia systems and accept a larger royal military presence on their territories. Between 1689 and 1748 the English-speaking colonies of North America fought three major conflicts against the French and their numerous native allies: King William's War (1689-1697), Queen Anne's War (1702-1713) and King George's War (1740-1748). The names of these conflicts derived from the monarchs who ruled England when they broke out; all these wars were nothing else than the "North American theatre" compared to the three major wars that ravaged Europe: The War of the Grand Alliance, The War of the Spanish Succession and The War of the Austrian Succession. They all ended without seeing significant changes in the political and military "balance of power" of North America, since the English-speaking colonies were never able to achieve a definitive victory over the French military forces stationed in Canada. The key moment in the long struggle between Britain and France for control of North America only came in 1754, when the French and Indian War broke out as part of the larger Seven Years' War that was fought in Europe. By 1750 the British colonial territories of North America had consolidated their political structures and were organized into thirteen independent entities, commonly known as the "Thirteen Colonies".

The Militias of the Thirteen Colonies

Each of the militias deployed by the Thirteen Colonies had its own peculiar history and organization, which was influenced by the strategic position of its home territory and by the main features of the latter's internal politics. The militias of some colonies, like those of Virginia and Massachusetts, had become consolidate institutions already during the 17th century; the militias of some "younger" colonies, instead, were still small by the outbreak of the American Revolution.

Virginia: Since the founding of Jamestown in 1607, it was clear to the Virginian colonists that if they wanted to survive in the New World, they had to organize themselves in some sort of military structure. In 1610 the Virginia militia received its first regular establishment, being organized into six companies or "bands" with 50 men each commanded by a captain. In addition, there was also a small "Guard of Halberdiers" escorting the royal governor. A training program was set up to ensure that all able-bodied colonists had to train and exercise regularly, with perfect military discipline. Each of the six companies in turn was on watch fully armed and equipped, while the others performed the daily activities required to the subsisting of the settlement. After 1622 the militia of Virginia was completely reorganized and started to be influenced by the system of the contemporary English "trained bands", albeit with some significant differences. In England, several householders could be grouped together in a single administrative unit and provide a single militiaman; in Virginia, instead, all settlers had to be armed. This practice, however, caused serious problems to the economic life of the colony since in case of war there would have been a chronic lack of workers in the fields. As a result, the following solution was adopted: each colonist who went on active service could rest assured that the other members of his community, who remained at home, would have performed the labours that were normally performed by him. Differently from what happened in England, where militiamen stored their weapons in local armouries or in the parish churches, in Virginia the militiamen kept their arms at home. In 1629 a further refinement was added to this general organization, with the division of Virginia into four military districts (each having a local commander). Militia forces from the different districts could operate together for combined operations, but also as separate corps to respond to local threats. Since 1651, the militia companies were assembled into county regiments; some years later, the territory of Virginia was divided into four provinces and nineteen counties. Each of the latter was to provide one regiment of infantry and one troop of horse. In addition to the militia forces, the royal governor also had a small personal guard that was commanded by a commissioned "Captain of the Guard". During Bacon's Rebellion, most of the militia supported the popular rising against the autocratic Governor William Berkeley. To crush the revolt as soon as possible, Charles II sent an English regular unit to the colony that was known as Jeffery's Regiment of Foot. When this unit went back to England, two independent companies of English regulars were formed to remain in Virginia. These, however, were soon disbanded in May 1682. During this period, the first small parties of "rangers" started to be organized inside the militia of Virginia. These, numbering around thirty men each, garrisoned the frontier forts and were mounted to travel long distances. They were paid in tobacco and had to provide their own arms, clothing, equipment, saddles, and horses. The general militia, instead, kept its county organization for several decades. At the outbreak of the French and Indian War the militia of Virginia comprised an impressive total of 30,000 men, but most of these were not trained and equipped in an effective way. Since July 1755, in order to defend the frontier areas of the colony from enemy raids, the local communities formed some units of volunteers to patrol the most exposed locations. These included several companies of infantry as well as two troops of light horse/mounted infantry. An additional cavalry unit, made up of two hundred volunteer "gentlemen", was also raised during the conflict. The members of all these corps were commonly known as "associators", since their corps were private associations formed on a voluntary basis and not militia units. In 1774, in Fairfax County, an independent infantry company was formed from volunteer militiamen. This was commanded by George Washington and was dressed in dark blue with buff facings; the latter uniform was later adopted as the standard dress of the new Continental Army.

Massachusetts: the settlement of Massachusetts in 1628 was relatively unopposed by the natives; from the outset, however, all able-bodied men of the new colony bore arms and were assembled into four companies. As the settlement expanded, new militia companies were organized; in order to give some proper training to these, in 1630 two military instructors were recruited. During the period October-December 1636, the militia companies of Massachusetts Bay Colony were re-ordered and formed into three regiments: the East, North and South Regiments. The East Regiment was the most important one, including militia companies from Boston and several other important centres. Despite this new organization, several independent "bands" continued to exist in the outlying communities of the colony. With the general growth in the number of militia units, there was a new need for specialized training. As a result, during 1637, there were proposals to set up in Boston a "special unit" that could provide training courses for militia officers and artillery services. The basic idea was that of creating something similar to the City of London's "Artillery Garden", which later became known as "Honourable Artillery Company". On 13 March 1638, the colonial authorities granted a charter for the creation of "The Military Company of Massachusetts", which first commander was the veteran Captain Robert Keayne (who had served in the London Company). Under Keayne's guidance, the new company became the first military training unit/artillery school of the American colonies. In 1643 the general organization of the militia was changed again, with the creation of new county regiments that bore the names of their respective counties. As in the rest of the other North American colonies, cavalry appeared in Massachusetts only later: this happened around 1650, when horses started to become increasingly common in New England and a first troop of horse was formed (which members were ordinary militiamen who acted as mounted soldiers only when their own county regiment was not in exercise). During the following years more troops of horses were formed: by 1667 there were twelve, with 160 cavalrymen each. The area of present-day Maine remained part of Massachusetts until 1820; as a result, its militia, which was composed by around 700 men in 1670, was organized into independent companies that were formally part of Massachusetts' militia. By 1676 the latter's strength was estimated at 40,000 able-bodied men, aged between 16 and 60 years of age. These trained eight times each year; in addition, each major town had some artillerymen who trained every week. In the following decades, because of the emergency faced during King Philip's War, the Massachusetts' militia continued to expand as the colony grew and more county regiments were formed. In 1744 a total of 150 militiamen from the various county regiments were chosen to form an independent company of grenadiers, which was attached to the York County Regiment. By the mid-18th century, the Military Company of Massachusetts had transformed itself into an independent militia company made up of Boston's most prominent merchants and had gradually lost its original functions. Meanwhile, a new "Train of Artillery" made up of volunteer gunners had been created to serve the guns of Boston. This unit was attached to the Boston Militia Regiment, together with an independent company of grenadiers. In 1728 a ceremonial military corps, known as Boston Cadet Company, had also been formed; this was to provide the escort for the governor of the colony and was made up of young gentlemen. A similar unit of "cadets" was later organized also in the city of Great Barrington. During 1754 the personal guard of the Massachusetts' governor was expanded with the formation of a "Company of Horse Guards", always made up of young gentlemen coming from Boston. In 1772 another ceremonial military unit was raised from the students at Harvard College, who were formally exempted from militia service; this consisted of an infantry company, which members were not permitted to bear arms.

New Hampshire: the first settlements established in New Hampshire dated back to 1623. Since the beginning, the settlers of this colony had to face serious military threats from the natives and the pirates who were active in the region. In 1631 a professional soldier was invited to the new settlements in order to organize the local militia and train the colonists. Ten years later, however, New Hampshire passed under the jurisdiction of Massachusetts and lost its autonomy. It became again independent only in 1679, when it was separated from Massachusetts by royal order. As a result, on 16 March 1680 the independent militia of New Hampshire was re-formed: this initially consisted of one infantry company for each of the four major settlements (Portsmouth, Dover, Exeter and Hampton), plus an artillery company and a troop of cavalry stationed in Portsmouth. The cavalry troop, however, was disbanded a few years later. With the progressive growing of the colony more militia companies were formed; in 1689 these were all grouped together in the so-called "New Hampshire Regiment of Militia". By 1730 the militia of New Hampshire was made up of two infantry regiments; these were supplemented, during the following decades, by some small independent detachments of "scouts" that were created to patrol the frontier areas. In 1748 these had a total of 174 men. In 1750 a troop of horse was raised from the inhabitants of Kingston and was added to the existing militia units. With the outbreak of the French and Indian War the New Hampshire militia was greatly expanded and came to comprise nine regiments of infantry as well as one regiment of cavalry. In 1773 another three infantry regiments were added to the militia, followed in 1775 by a ceremonial "Company of Cadets".

Connecticut: 250 colonists led by Thomas Hooker, coming from Massachusetts, settled on the west bank of the Connecticut River in early 1636. One of the reasons why Hooker had left Massachusetts Bay Colony was that only members of the Puritan Church could vote and participate in the government of the colony; he believed, instead, that any adult male owning property should have had the right to vote and take part to the political life of his community. No militia was initially formed by the Connecticut colonists, but relations with the local natives soon became increasingly difficult. As a result, the settlers were ordered to assemble for training once a month and were organized in companies; by 1650 these included approximately 800 men and were supplemented by a troop of horse raised in Hartford during 1658. Following the Dutch recapture of New York in 1673, Connecticut's colonial authorities ordered that 500 militiamen (a third of the colony's militia at that time) had to be mounted to patrol the coast. During King Philip's War, Connecticut contributed to the war efforts of New England by sending a force of 315 militiamen. In addition, 350 militia "dragoons" (mounted infantrymen) were employed against the natives; these men had to provide horses, weapons, equipment and clothes for themselves but could be compensated by the colonial authorities in case of loss of their properties. During the middle part of Queen Anne's War, 800 Connecticut militiamen patrolled the frontier of their colony (on horseback during summer, on snowshoes during winter). In 1739 the Connecticut militia was reorganized into thirteen infantry regiments, formed by assembling the companies raised in the various settlements. Each of these regiments was to have an attached cavalry troop. During this same period the students at Yale College organized an artillery company that was known as "College Artillery". Some years later, another independent artillery company was organized in New London. Finally, during 1769, an elite infantry company known as "The Governor's Foot Guard" was also raised (followed by a second company of the same kind in 1771).

Rhode Island: in January 1636, Salem minister Roger Williams was banished from Massachusetts because of his theological differences with the ruling class of the colony. He preached that government and religion should be separated and believed that the natives had been treated by the English settlers with no justice. After being exiled from Massachusetts, Williams bought some land for establishing a new colony in present-day Providence, Rhode Island. Williams and his group of colonists settled at the tip of Narragansett Bay and the new site was called "Providence Plantation" (which soon became a place of religious freedom). Since the early days of the Providence settlement, the Rhode Island colonists gave much importance to their military organization but had very few opportunities to gain some combat experience. Some volunteer units of cavalry and artillery, including the "Island Troop of Horse" formed in 1667 at Newport and disbanded after a few years, were gradually added to the original infantry companies: the Providence Troop of Horse (1719), the King's County Troop of Horse (1730), the Artillery Company of Newport (1741), the Artillery Company of Providence (1744), the 1st Newport Troop of Horse (1746), the Westerly/Charlestown Artillery Company (1755), the Newport Infantry Company (1755) and the 2nd Newport Troop of Horse (1760). In 1774 the Artillery Company of Providence was transformed into a ceremonial unit known as "Providence Cadet Company" that was made up of young gentlemen. In 1774, because of the growing political discontent, several new independent companies of militiamen were organized: Providence Light Infantry, Providence Grenadier Company, Providence Fusiliers, North Providence Rangers, Providence Artillery Company, Gloucester Light Infantry, Pawtuxet Rangers, Newport Light Infantry and Kentish Guards.

Maryland: the colony of Maryland was founded in 1634 by a group of English Catholic refugees, under a charter obtained from King Charles I. By 1638 the St. Mary Colony had its own "trained band" of militiamen numbering 120 men. During the following years, the militia was expanded and thus received a better organization: in the early 1640s, for example, captains were appointed for "every hundred" men. In April 1650, the Maryland legislative assembly ordered the establishment of a small full-time garrison of six men (under a captain) in the strategic fort located at St. Inigo Harbour. In March 1655 Maryland saw the beginning of a strong internal clash between Puritan and Catholic

Maryland Puritan "Associators" militia at the Battle of the Mouth of the Severn in 1689. (John E.Kelly, New York Public Library, 1876).

settlers, which ended with the victory of the former at the Battle of the Severn River. After the end of the hostilities, the militia was ordered to disarm any inhabitant suspected of disaffection towards the colony's new Puritan government. As a result, Catholics, Quakers, and Baptists were disarmed and their rights of citizenship were denied. On 12 July 1658, the independent militia companies of Maryland were assembled into two regiments, respectively known as the "Northern" and the "Southern" Regiments. In addition, there was also an independent "Governor's Own Company", which performed guard duties. With the progressive expansion of the colony new county regiments of militia were organized, which included troops of cavalry and dragoons in addition to the usual foot companies. Since 1692, a certain number of rangers started to be posted to the forts built along the frontier with native territories. With the outbreak of the French and Indian War, the militia of Maryland was expanded with the formation of some volunteer units that were tasked with patrolling the frontier with the territories inhabited by the natives. These corps, however, were all quite short-lived. In 1774 a ceremonial company of Independent Cadets was raised from the gentlemen of Baltimore.

New York: this colony, which had been previously known as "New Netherland" since it had been created by the Dutch, came firmly under English control in 1674. The Militia Act of 1677 prescribed the raising of 6,000 militiamen organized into several independent companies, 2,000 of whom were to be mounted. Very soon, however, this large number of militia cavalry became impossible to sustain from an economic point of view and was rapidly reduced. In November 1700 the militia of New York mustered a total of 3,182 men, organized in eight county regiments: City and County of New York, the City and County of Albany, Suffolk, Queen's, King's, Richmond, West Chester and the combined counties of Ulster and Duchess. In addition to these infantry regiments there were mounted units in New York, Albany, Queen's, King's, Ulster and Duchess Counties. During the period 1700-1770 the militia of New York was gradually expanded with the formation of several new units; shortly before the outbreak of the American Revolution, it comprised the following corps: 26 regiments of infantry, 11 troops of cavalry and some independent companies of artillery (for a total of 32,000 men). The best of the few artillery companies was that stationed in New York, also known as "Blue Company ", from the colour of its uniform. Some units made up of volunteers did also exist, plus one independent company of grenadiers in New York ("The New York City Grenadiers") and a similar one in Albany.

New Jersey: this colony became predominantly inhabited by English settlers only since 1664. Being under no serious military threat and having a very small population, it developed its militia units quite slowly. A Militia Act passed in 1730 improved the general organization of the few existing companies. By the 1750's the militia was formed into the 1st New Jersey Regiment (The Jersey Blues)

The New Jersey Blues from the 1750's (NJ Militia Museum).

to guard against native American raids and saw service in New York during the French-Indian War where the unit was decimated in the defence of Fort William Henry. The corps was soon reorganized and made up the majority of New Jersey's militia until the outbreak of the Revolution. In addition to the Jersey Blues there also was a state-chartered corps, the Frontier Guard, that was tasked with patrolling the course of the Delaware (especially when the Blues were out of the state).

Pennsylvania: the first English settlers arrived in Pennsylvania during the late 1660s and organized a small militia in 1669. The few able-bodied men of the early settlements later came under the New York militia law in 1676, thus having no independent militia structure. The real colonization of Pennsylvania, however, only started in 1681 when the territory was chartered to William Penn of the "Society of Friends" (a religious group commonly known in England as the "Quakers"). Quakers were pacifists, who believed that no man could kill another one for any reason. Being persecuted in England for their religious beliefs, they followed the example of the Puritans and obtained the charter for a territory in North America. The "Commonwealth of Pennsylvania" was a real anomaly among the English colonies of North America in that it had no military forces and no militia laws. A few of Pennsylvania's early settlers were not Quakers and thus bore arms for personal defence, but they were a minority. Attempts to raise volunteers from this colony during Queen Anne's War failed completely and the first militia units of Pennsylvania were only raised in 1744. These were quite different from those of the other colonies, since they consisted of volunteers who were paid by the colonial government for their weapons and for some other expenses. These volunteers were assembled into small companies with 50 or 100 men each. In 1747 a young Benjamin Franklin contributed to raising one such volunteer unit, by organizing a corps of 600 men assembled into 11 infantry companies. This was known as the "Associated Regiment of Philadelphia" and its members were called "The Associators". Very soon a similar regiment, with 9 infantry companies, was raised from the countryside of Philadelphia. Benjamin Franklin's example was later followed in all the counties of Pennsylvania and the following "Associated" corps were organized: one regiment with 33 companies in Lancaster County, one regiment with 26 companies in Chester County and one regiment with 18 companies in Buck's County. The Associated Regiment of Philadelphia comprised also two companies of artillery, which were tasked with manning the two batteries that protected their city. With the end of King George's War, however, the "Associated" corps were all disbanded and the interesting military experiment organized by Benjamin Franklin came to an end. In 1755 the first Militia Law of Pennsylvania was approved, but this did not change the existing situation in a significant way since service in the militia remained voluntary. During 1756 one infantry company and one artillery company, having permanent character, were raised for service in Philadelphia. These were later supplemented by another company of infantry and by a single troop of cavalry. The new Militia Law passed in 1757 made military service in the militia compulsory also for Pennsylvania, but this was never put in practice. As a result, to defend at least the frontier settlements from native raiders, one volunteer company of rangers had to be organized during 1763. In that same period a unit of volunteer frontiersmen, known as "Paxton Boys", was also formed to fight against the natives. The latter had a semi-regular status and massacred many natives without a good reason: as a result, they were soon disbanded after menacing to march on the city of Philadelphia. To face the "Paxton Boys", Benjamin Franklin reformed the Associated Regiment of Philadelphia; the latter now had 1,000 volunteers in six companies of infantry, two companies of cavalry and one company of artillery. After these events, the Associated Regiment was again disbanded; it was reformed only in 1775, in view of the outbreak of the American Revolution. During 1774, because of political discontent, some independent volunteer corps were raised: the Philadelphia Greens, the Quaker Blues and the Troop of Light Horse.

Delaware: originally settled by Swedes, Delaware later became part of New Netherland Colony with the rest of New Sweden. Following the English conquest of 1664, Delaware became part of New York Colony. During this period the colonial settlements of Delaware were quite small and had very few inhabitants. Since 1669, some militia companies were organized as part of New York's larger militia; in 1682, however, Delaware was separated from New York and absorbed into Pennsylvania. William Penn allowed the area to have its own legislative assembly, which soon made Delaware an autonomous colony. Having different religious beliefs from the Quakers of Pennsylvania, the settlers of Delaware always continued to have their own independent companies of militia. The latter remained very few until 1775, since the population of the colony was quite small.

North Carolina: the territories of the future colonies of Georgia, North Carolina and South Carolina were granted as a single "Carolina Colony" since 1629. English expansion over these southern areas was not very fast, with real colonization taking place only during the 1670s. According to the 1669 Constitution of Carolina, all able-bodied men aged between 17 and 60 had to bear arms and serve into the militia when necessary. Two militia companies were soon formed, which gradually expanded over the years due to the menace represented by the local natives. In 1673 a cavalry unit known as "Governor's Horse Guard" was formed. By 1685 the military of Carolina included two militia regiments (named "Northward" and "Southward") and the cavalry troop known as "Governor's Horse Guard". Later, an independent militia company was also added: this was made up of Huguenots (Protestants) who had fled from France because of the religious persecutions organized against them by Louis XIV. According to the 1696 Militia Act, companies were to drill at least every two months and regiments were to assemble once a year. When the Spanish and the French attacked Charleston in 1706, during Queen Anne's War, the local militia of what would later become South Carolina included 1,500 men: two companies from Charleston, seven from the "Northward Regiment" and one from the "Southward Regiment". In 1704 the so-called "Patrol Act" ordered that ten men from each militia company had to serve on horse, in order to patrol their districts and prevent enemy raids or slave uprisings. In 1710 Carolina's territory was divided into North and South Carolina; in the former, which was sparsely inhabited, the first militia law was passed only in 1715. Despite this, the militia of North Carolina was not mobilized until 1754; during the French and Indian War, however, it could muster just a few men having superficial training and with outdated equipment. Since 1764 some small corps of rangers were formed to patrol the frontier areas of the colony, but the general situation of the militia did not change until the outbreak of the American Revolution.

South Carolina: in 1710 the organization of this colony's militia was still the same as 1706, with 1,500 men. The elite "Governor's Horse Guard" became part of South Carolina's military units. In 1716 the latter were supplemented by two independent companies of mounted rangers, which were tasked with patrolling the western frontier of the colony. Since 1719 trusted black slaves were authorised to serve in the militia, something exceptional in the military history of the Thirteen Colonies. Acts of bravery from the black militiamen could be rewarded with the granting of freedom to the individual who had distinguished himself in combat. In 1740, however, this "social experiment" came to an end after the failure of a large slave revolt. During 1739 a second troop of the "Governor's Horse Guard" had been raised, followed by a third one in 1740 and by a fourth one in 1743. At the beginning of King George's War, the militia of South Carolina comprised five infantry regiments, which were later

Officer of the South Carolina Militia, wearing pre-war uniform (left) and militiaman of the South Carolina Militia, wearing hunting shirt (right). *Photo by Dr. Eric Nason, 2ⁿᵈ South Carolina Regiment. (Courtesy of the ASKB)*

augmented to seven (having a total of 92 companies). By 1774 another five regiments had been added to this general establishment. In 1760 seven independent companies (with 75 mounted rangers each) were raised from volunteer militiamen, but these were all disbanded by 1762. During 1765-1766 the Charleston Regiment had two additional companies, one of grenadiers and one of light infantry; both were disbanded quite soon, but the light infantry one was later re-formed in 1773. Since 1750 the "Governor's Horse Guard" assumed the new denomination of "Regiment of Horse Militia" and was reduced to just three troops. In 1756 some gentlemen from Charleston organized a volunteer artillery company; finally, during 1761, a small constabulary corps known as "Watch Company" was also formed to keep order in Charleston.

Georgia: this colony was created in 1733, as a buffer between Spanish Florida and South Carolina. Its militia started to be organized in a proper way only after the end of King George's War, when four independent companies of volunteers were raised in Savannah (three of infantry and one of artillery). A single company of rangers, patrolling the frontier, existed since 1734. In 1739, due to the outbreak of hostilities with Spain, another two units of rangers were formed: The Troop of English Rangers and the Troop of Highland Rangers. These were later supplemented by a Highland Independent Company of Foot. As clear from their name, the two Highland corps were recruited from Scottish settlers. In 1740 a Marine Company of Boatmen was created to patrol the hinterland waterways of Georgia. During the French and Indian War the ordinary infantry companies were increased to eight, but after the end of the hostilities the militia of Georgia remained very small until the outbreak of the American Revolution. Shortly before the latter, in 1773, an independent troop of mounted rangers was formed.

A member of the New Jersey Blues in marching order, 1758. (*Knotel courtesy of the NYPL*)

The Provincial Troops

Between 1700 and 1750 the British military presence in North America had become more significant but was still quite small. This was the situation in each of the colonies that had a royal garrison:
-   New York: four independent companies of infantry, raised in 1694 and disbanded in 1763.
-   South Carolina: one independent company of infantry, made up of veteran soldiers, existed during 1721-1736 in order to protect the colony from the incursions of the Spanish troops garrisoning Florida. Four independent companies of infantry were sent to Charlestown during the years of King George's War.

This situation came to an end only in 1754, when significant British regular military forces started to be sent to the Americas in order to fight in the French-Indian War. It is interesting to note, however, that the British Army recruited several regiments in the Thirteen Colonies even before 1754. These were the following:

-   Oglethorpe's 42nd Regiment of Foot: raised in Georgia during 1737 and disbanded in 1748.
-   Gooch's 61st Regiment of Foot: raised from all the American colonies in 1740 and having a large establishment with four battalions. It was disbanded in 1746.
-   Shirley's Regiment of Foot: raised in New England during 1745 to garrison the fortress of Louisbourg, captured from the French during King George's War. It was disbanded in 1749.
-   Pepperell's Regiment of Foot: raised in New England during 1745 to garrison the fortress of Louisbourg, captured from the French during King George's War. It was disbanded in 1749.

When the French and Indian War began, the authorities of the Thirteen Colonies were forced to recruit large numbers of new military units in addition to their ordinary militia ones. The new conflict, in fact, was fought on a large scale and most its operations took place in remote areas of North America. The militia units were organized and trained to fight for only short periods of time and not far from their home territories; as a result, a new category of American military forces had to be created. These were the so-called "Provincial Troops" or "Provincials", permanent full-time corps that were available for conducting extended operations far from their home colony. Most of the new Provincial units were recruited through a quota system that was applied to the existing militia; generally speaking, they were made up of the best militiamen who were interested in having a military career. The Provincials had a lot in common with the regular regiments of the British Army but were "temporary" corps, which were usually disbanded when the campaign or war for which they had been formed came to an end. In this sense, they were similar to the original militia units. Some early Provincial Troops had already been organized during the 1745 expedition against the French fortress of Louisbourg; on that occasion, in fact, the following units were formed:

- Massachusetts: seven infantry regiments
- New Hampshire: one infantry regiment
- Connecticut: one infantry regiment
- Rhode Island: three infantry companies

NCO of the English independent companies garrisoning South Carolina (left) and two members of the famous Rogers' Rangers (right), from the years of the French and Indian War.

Following the capture of Louisbourg, the American colonies decided to assemble a larger military force in order to attempt an invasion of Canada. This ended up as a failure, but led to the formation of the following units:

- Massachusetts: two infantry regiments with a total of 27 companies
- Connecticut: one infantry regiment with a total of 10 companies
- New Hampshire: one infantry regiment with a total of 9 companies
- Rhode Island: 3 independent infantry companies
- New York: 31 independent infantry companies
- New Jersey: 5 independent infantry companies
- Maryland: 3 independent infantry companies
- Pennsylvania: 4 independent infantry companies
- Virginia: 1 independent infantry company

The number of Provincials units raised during the French and Indian War was much larger than the allocated numbers which was impressive for the American standards of the time. Each of the Thirteen Colonies, in fact, contributed to the war effort.

Connecticut: the first two infantry regiments were raised in 1755, followed by another two during the same year. In 1757 another temporary infantry regiment was added, which was disbanded in 1758. The original four units were maintained until 1761 when they were reduced to two regiments supplemented by two independent infantry companies. All corps were disbanded in 1763.

Delaware: 300 Provincials were raised for the campaign of 1758.

Georgia: this colony provided only two companies of rangers and one troop of cavalry, due to its limited population.

Maryland: in 1754 a single company of rangers was mobilized, followed by 200 Provincials having garrison duties. During 1755 an infantry battalion was organized.

Massachusetts: initially this colony raised a single infantry regiment having two independent battalions. During 1755 another two infantry regiments with 500 men each were organized, together with a small "train of artillery" consisting of the following elements: one captain, one lieutenant, one assistant, three NCOs and 16 gunners. For the campaign of 1756, the Provincials of Massachusetts were greatly expanded and were reorganized in the following corps: seven infantry regiments with 500 soldiers each and two artillery companies with 110 men each. In 1757 the infantry was reduced to a single regiment, having a large establishment with 1,800 soldiers in 17 companies. In 1758 Massachusetts' war effort reached its peak, with the raising of seven infantry regiments having 1,000 men each. In 1759 the Provincial infantry of this colony was reorganized on eight regiments and four independent companies. These were supplemented by 300 pioneers having auxiliary duties. During 1760 the infantry regiments were reduced to five and then to three in 1761. In addition to the above, since 1757, a small independent infantry company was garrisoned in Boston.

New Hampshire: initially the Provincials of New Hampshire consisted of two infantry regiments, one independent infantry company having garrison duties and one company of rangers. In 1756 the foot regiments were reduced to one and the ranger company was re-formed. During 1757 one battalion and one independent company of infantry were added to the existing units, both having garrison duties. A single company of carpenters and three companies of rangers were also raised. From 1758 to 1760 New Hampshire continued to provide a single infantry regiment to the British war effort.

New Jersey: at the beginning of the hostilities this colony organized a single battalion of infantry and a "Frontier Guard" made up of 400 soldiers. During 1756 the infantry unit was expanded and became a regiment; in 1757, instead, a new company of rangers was formed. Before the end of the hostilities, in 1762, New Jersey also contributed with the creation of an independent infantry company having garrison duties.

New York: in 1755 a single regiment of infantry was organized, which was re-raised for the campaigns of 1756 and 1757. During 1758 the establishment of this single unit was expanded to three battalions. In 1759 the original New York Regiment was reduced to two battalions, but in 1760 another three short-lived infantry regiments were formed.

North Carolina: at the outbreak of the French and Indian War this colony raised a single (weak) regiment of infantry. This was soon supplemented by a ranger company and by a small garrison company (tasked with frontier defence). Later another three independent infantry companies were formed and were assembled with the existing one in order to organize a battalion. In 1757 the Provincials of North Carolina were reduced to just two independent companies with 50 men each; during the following year, however, a new infantry battalion was raised (which continued to be supported by two garrison companies). In 1759 only the latter remained active, each having just 30 men. During 1761 an infantry regiment with seven companies was raised, but this was quite short-lived.

Pennsylvania: in 1754 this colony had no proper militia to speak of, since it had always been dominated by pacifist Quakers. An organization of volunteers, created by Benjamin Franklin and known as "Associated Companies", provided military services to the colony's government. Very soon, however, three Provincial infantry battalions were raised in Pennsylvania in order to fight against the French. In 1757 these were reduced to two and were grouped into a single regiment. During 1758 a third battalion was re-formed, and the internal establishment of all battalions was expanded (the first had 12 companies, the second 13 and the third had 17). The first two battalions also had an attached troop of cavalry.

Rhode Island: this colony initially contributed with a single infantry regiment, which was re-raised in 1756. During the latter year a second infantry regiment, with 400 soldiers, was also organized. In 1757 the establishment with two infantry regiments was confirmed and one company of rangers was also added. In addition, one "reserve" battalion with 250 men was organized (this was to be used only in case of need). During 1758-1760 Rhode Island contributed to the British war effort with a single infantry regiment, which maintained a standard establishment of 1,000 soldiers.

South Carolina: the first Provincials of this territory were raised only in 1760, when seven troops of mounted rangers were formed to fight against the natives along the frontier. Soon afterwards a small infantry regiment was organized, which continued to serve until 1761.

A young George Washington wearing that dark blue uniform with red facings of the Virginia Regiment, one of the many "provincial" military units formed during the French and Indian War. (Charles Wilson Peale, 1772, Washington & Lee University)

Virginia: in 1754 this colony raised its first Provincial military unit, the famous Virginia Regiment that was later commanded by the young Colonel George Washington. This soon proved to be an excellent unit and participated to the Braddock's Expedition of 1755. During the latter, at the Battle of Monongahela, the Virginia Regiment (with ten companies) was annihilated and suffered severe losses. Virginia contributed to the military operations in the Ohio River Valley also with six companies of foot rangers, one company of mounted rangers and two companies of carpenters. The Virginia Regiment was rapidly re-raised, this time with an expanded establishment of 16 companies. In 1758 a Second Virginia Regiment was formed, while the original one remained under command of Colonel Washington. In 1759 the new regiment was disbanded and a "reserve" force of 500 soldiers was organized. Before the end of the French and Indian War, three independent companies of "frontier guards" were also raised.

      With the end of the war with France, most of the Provincial units listed above very rapidly disbanded by the authorities of the various colonies. The new kind of troops represented by the Provincials, however, continued to exist (albeit on a smaller scale) until the outbreak of the American Revolution. The direct heirs of the Provincial units in the latter conflict were the so-called "State Troops" of the single colonies and the "Loyalist Corps" supporting the British Army. The creation of the Provincials, for the first time in American history, had demonstrated that the Thirteen Colonies could field substantial military contingents also for long periods of service.

      During King George's War and the French and Indian War, various ranger units were raised in the Thirteen Colonies. Some of these were quite different from those created inside the state militias during the first half of the 18th century, because their members were not only tasked with patrolling the countryside but also to act as an elite "shock force" designed for special operations. The early company of rangers created by Benjamin Church during King Philip's War, in 1675, already had this distinctive character; the latter, however, was progressively lost after the hostilities with Metacomet came to an end and after this first company of rangers was temporarily disbanded. Benjamin Church's rangers of 1675-1676 consisted of 200 volunteers assembled into an independent company; 60 of these were colonists while the remaining 140 were friendly natives. The latter trained their white companions and transmitted to them all the needed skills related to bush fighting. Benjamin Church was an experienced scout and woodland fighter, who had understood that the only way to obtain some decisive victories against the natives was to fight by using their same combat tactics. His company of rangers, in fact, was created to penetrate deeply in the enemy territory in order to conduct retaliatory raids or to gather some precious intelligence about the movements of the natives. Church's men were all equipped as light infantrymen, like their native opponents. They wore comfortable moccasins in order to walk or run rapidly in the woods and were armed with hatches in order to perform hand-to-hand fighting against native warriors armed with tomahawks. They moved on horseback when possible and were also trained to sail on canoes. All rangers were excellent marksmen and were able to reload their muskets very rapidly. During King William's War and Queen Anne's War the independent company of rangers guided by Benjamin Church was reformed, but it always remained a temporary corps and thus was definitively disbanded after Church's retirement from military service. During 1710-1713 another short-lived unit of rangers, made up of friendly Mohawk natives commanded by two white officers, was created to garrison Port-Royal in Nova Scotia. It was not until 1744, however, that another unit of "rangers" in the true sense of the word was formed.

In 1744 three small companies of "Nova Scotia Rangers", each with 60 men, were raised in Massachusetts and were sent to Nova Scotia in order to reinforce the local garrison. The latter was particularly exposed to the frequent attacks of the local native tribes, who were loyal allies of the French. Nova Scotia had previously been part of the French dominions of North America with the name of Acadia and thus the French always nurtured the ambition of reconquering it. On the border of Nova Scotia there were some Jesuit missions, which the French used as their logistical bases to coordinate the raids of their native allies directed against the English settlements. The "Nova Scotia Rangers" were specifically created to face the menace represented by the French and by their native allies; they soon became known as "Goreham's Rangers", from the name of their skilled commander. Most members of these three companies were Mohawks or individuals of mixed heritage who did know very well how to fight in the difficult environment of Nova Scotia. Very soon the original three companies were reduced to one, which had a larger establishment with 130 rangers and 8 officers. The Goreham's Rangers served with distinction during the French and Indian War, to the point of being made part of the British Army's regular establishment with the new denomination of "North American Rangers". Goreham's men were the first rangers to receive this honour in the military history of Colonial America. The corps was also expanded to two companies, one garrisoned in Nova Scotia and one in New Brunswick. With the end of the French and Indian War, in 1763, the North American Rangers were disbanded.

In 1755, after the outbreak of the French and Indian War, the most famous unit of colonial rangers was formed in New Hampshire: the "Roger's Rangers". These originated from a single company that was detached from one of the ordinary militia regiments to perform scouting duties, which was commanded by Captain Robert Rogers. By the spring of 1756, the new unit had already showed all its great potential and consisted of one captain, one lieutenant, one ensign, three sergeants and 60 rangers. From a formal point of view, Roger's Rangers were a "Provincial" unit that was re-enlisted every year; differently from the other Provincials, however, they were paid by the British government. During 1756 the corps was greatly expanded, with the formation of another four companies (one of which was entirely made up of friendly Stockbridge natives). At the beginning of 1757, the internal composition of the single companies was increased as follows: one captain, one lieutenant, one ensign, four

The mortally wounded Edward Braddock during Braddock's Retreat, 1755

sergeants and 100 rangers. During 1757 the number of companies was increased to nine; the rangers were so effective in their scouting operations that their commander Robert Roger was ordered to train one company of British regulars (as volunteers) as he did with his own rangers. In 1758 another six companies of rangers, always paid by the British Crown, were raised in New England; two of these were made up of friendly Stockbridge natives. In November 1760, with the fall of French Canada, all the companies of rangers returned to New England and were disbanded shortly afterwards except for two ones that continued to serve until 1761.

Very soon the British government understood that some corps of rangers were absolutely needed in North America, to contrast the military initiatives of the native tribes. As a result, in 1762, Captain Joseph Hopkins was ordered to raise a new corps of rangers from Maryland and Pennsylvania. This new unit would have been known as "Queen's Royal American Rangers" and would have been placed on the regular establishment of the British Army. It consisted of two officers and 100 men, thus having the numerical consistency of a company. The Queen's Royal American Rangers played a prominent role during the so-called "Pontiac's Rebellion", which commenced shortly after Canada was included into the British colonial possessions. Most of the native tribes that had fought with the French during the French and Indian War, in fact, had no intention to accept British rule over their lands. The new corps of rangers was disbanded at the end of 1763; it was the last "true" ranger unit to be formed in North America until the beginning of the American Revolution.

The Birth of the Continental Army

When the American Revolution began, in April 1775, the Thirteen Colonies could count only on their militias to fight against the British regulars who were stationed on their territory. The general number of the latter had been significantly enlarged during the previous ten years and thus the British military presence in North America was no longer a small one as it had been until the French and Indian War. In the early phase of the Revolution the American militiamen were able to obtain some victories over the British redcoats, by using the effective hit-and-run guerrilla tactics that were typical of the "minutemen". Very soon, however, it became clear that the conflict with Great Britain going to be very long and difficult; as a result, the Americans needed to form a regular military force that could be used for large-scale conventional operations against the British. Since the beginning George Washington supported the idea of creating a "common army", which would have been made up of units recruited from all the Thirteen Colonies. Initially there was some strong resistance to this proposed plan, since most of the colonies were jealous of their autonomy and did not want to replace their militias with a permanent military organization. The First Continental Congress of 1774 had already rejected the proposal of creating a standing army, but the military events of early 1775 changed the situation. On 14 June 1775, in fact, the Second Continental Congress ordered the organization of a unified "Continental Army". The nucleus of the latter would have been formed by the thousands of militiamen who had already assembled themselves around Boston (22,000) and New York (5,000). The Congress elected George Washington as Commander-in-Chief of the new Continental Army by unanimous vote. The first unit in this new army became an elite regiment, known as 1st Continental Regiment, which would have been recruited from chosen riflemen of three different colonies (Pennsylvania, Maryland and Virginia). This unit, with ten companies, was to have a light infantry character and was to function as a "model" for all the other ones that had to be formed: in fact, it was made up of soldiers coming from different colonies and not of militiamen raised from a single colony. Initially the 1st Continental Regiment was to comprise six companies from Pennsylvania, two from Maryland and two from Virginia; in the end, however, the Pennsylvania volunteers wishing to serve in the new corps were so many that it had to be expanded

George Washington taking command of the Continental Army in 1775 (*C. Rogers 1822*)

to 13 companies (nine from Pennsylvania, two from Maryland and two from Virginia). On paper the new Continental Army was supposed to have been comprised of 39 regiments of infantry plus one regiment and two independent companies of artillery. Each of the Thirteen Colonies had to contribute to its formation, by providing the following units:

- Massachusetts: 27 regiments
- New York: 5 regiments
- Connecticut: 3 regiments
- New Hampshire: 3 regiments
- Rhode Island: 3 regiments
- Virginia: 2 regiments, plus 2 companies for the 1st Continental Regiment
- North Carolina: 2 regiments
- South Carolina: 2 regiments
- Pennsylvania: 1 regiment (the 1st Continental Regiment)
- Maryland: no regiments, just 2 companies for the 1st Continental Regiment
- Georgia: 1 regiment, the formation of which was only completed during 1776

The artillery regiment, known as Continental Artillery Regiment, was raised in Massachusetts; the two independent companies of artillery, instead, were provided by New York and Rhode Island. All infantry regiments were to have ten, line companies, while the artillery one was to have ten batteries (later increased to eleven). During 1776 also the independent artillery company of Rhode Island was absorbed into the Continental Artillery Regiment, bringing the total of companies in the latter to twelve.

Most of the units listed above were deployed in the Boston area and were grouped into three divisions with two infantry brigades each. In the New York area there were just seven infantry regiments and the independent artillery company of New York, supplemented by two independent corps: the Green Mountain Rangers from Vermont (at that time still part of New York Colony) and the New Hampshire Rangers. The former unit had been created in 1764, as part of the militia units recruited from the communities of Vermont. Initially this corps was known as the Green Mountain Boys and was formed to support Vermont's claims for independence from New York Colony. When the American Revolution broke out, however, the Green Mountain Boys adopted the new denomination of Green Mountain Rangers and joined the Continental Army. The corps had the establishment of a line infantry regiment but was trained like a light infantry unit: its commander, Colonel Seth Warner, had served in the famous Roger's Rangers during the French and Indian War and thus had some vast experience of bush fighting. Members of the Green Mountain Rangers were allowed to elect all their officers, including the superior ones; as a result, this unit was a sort of democratic "brotherhood" and not a simple regiment. With the progression of time, after being absorbed into the Continental Army, the Green Mountain Rangers started to be simply known as "Warner's Regiment". This unit was disbanded in 1781. During the American Revolution Vermont had a very peculiar political position: in 1777 it declared its independence from both Great Britain and the New York Colony; as a result, it became a sort of "neutral" territory where deserters of the opposing armies could find asylum. After the end of the American Revolution, Vermont continued to ask for its autonomy and was finally able to achieve the latter only in 1791 (when it became a state). The New Hampshire Rangers initially consisted of just one company but were later expanded with the addition of another eight companies; they were recruited from the frontiersmen of northern New Hampshire and were tasked with the protection of their home territory. Like the Green Mountain Rangers, also the New Hampshire Rangers joined the Continental military forces in New York. After being expanded, the corps assumed the new denomination of "Bedel's Regiment"; it was officially disbanded in January 1777.

The uniforms of the Continental Army in one of Richard Knotel's famous plates. The figure in the centre, with black round hat and white hunting shirt, is from the Provisional Rifle Corps.

In June 1775 the Continental military forces stationed around New York were ordered to invade the Canadian province of Quebec, in the hope of convincing the local settlers to join the revolutionary cause. At that time Quebec was still mostly inhabited by French settlers, who had been obliged to accept British rule only after France was defeated in the French and Indian War. The Americans were sure that the colonists of Quebec would revolt against the British and that they would join the Continental Army; against the odds, instead, the French-speaking Canadians remained loyal to the British Crown and fought with great determination to defend Quebec from the American invasion. This invasion in October 1776, was a complete failure. It should be noted, however, that a certain number of Canadians effectively decided to join the Continental Army during the American invasion of Quebec and that these formed two infantry regiments. The 1st Canadian Regiment was organized by James Livingston in September 1776 and was officially recognized as part of the Continental

HEADQUARTER AND STAFF
1779 - 1781

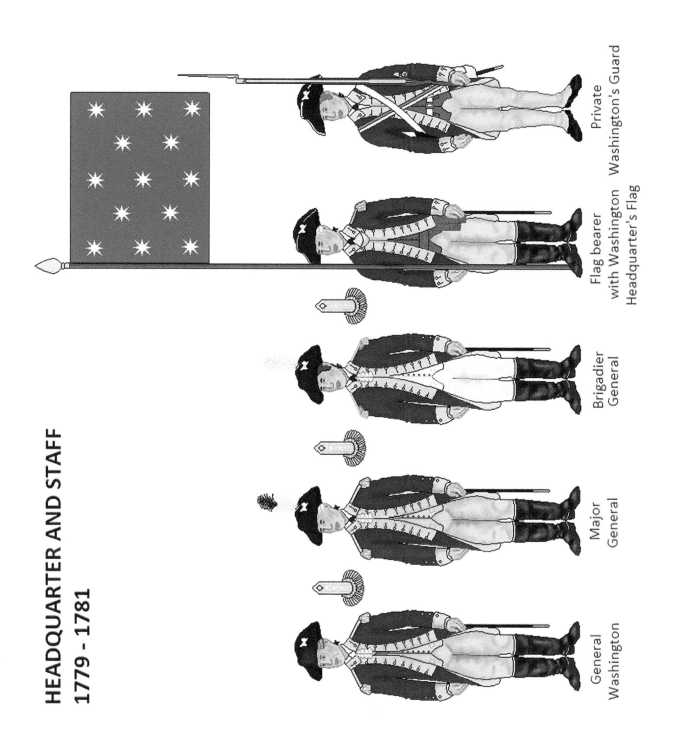

Private Washington's Guard

Flag bearer with Washington Headquarter's Flag

Brigadier General

Major General

General Washington

Private
Sherburne's additional
Continental Regiment
1777

3rd New-Jersey
Battalion
1776

private
3rd Regiment
New York 1776

Lee's additional
Continental
Regiment 1777

Army during November of the same year. Like some other units that we will analyse below, it was considered to be an "extra" unit attached to the Continental military forces; as such, it was under direct control of the Continental Congress and not of any of the Thirteen Colonies. Like all other line units of the Continental Army, this regiment had an establishment of ten companies totalling 1,000 soldiers (which could be found only on paper). When the American invasion of Quebec failed, the 1st Canadian Regiment followed the Continental Army in its retreat. During 1778-1780 it was kept as a garrison unit in New York as a "reserve" unit and played a crucial part in unmasking Benedict Arnold's treachery. The corps was finally disbanded at the beginning of 1781. The formation of a 2nd Canadian Regiment was authorized by the Continental Congress in January 1776; this new unit, like the other Canadian corps, would have been under direct control of the Congress and thus soon started to be known as "The Congress' Own Regiment". It was to have a large establishment with four battalions of five companies each, being the only over-sized unit of the Continental Army. Commanded by Moses Hazen, it was formed by recruiting Canadian volunteers and refugees who had supported the American invasion of Quebec. The 2nd Canadian Regiment, despite never reaching its planned establishment, served with distinction on several occasions and absorbed the remnants of the 1st Canadian Regiment when this was disbanded. After assuming the designation of "Canadian Regiment" in January 1781 and absorbing all the foreigners of the Continental Army, it continued to serve until being disbanded in 1783.

Uniforms of the Continental Army's infantry and light dragoons. As clear from this picture, before the introduction of the first dress regulations in 1779, the military forces under Washington's command presented a varied appearance.

Most of the units of the Continental Army had been enlisted by the Second Continental Congress for a period of service of just 12 months; as a result, at the beginning of 1776, the military forces under command of George Washington had to be re-enlisted and were partly reorganized. According to the new general structure prescribed in January 1776, the Continental Army was to be comprised of twenty-seven-line infantry regiments with eight companies each; these were provided by the various colonies/states as follows:

- Massachusetts: 16 regiments
- Connecticut: 5 regiments
- New Hampshire: 3 regiments
- Rhode Island: 2 regiments
- Pennsylvania: 1 regiment

(Left) An American soldier pictured in a German manuscript of the period, dressed in the rifleman's outfit, with a leather mitre hat and the words "Congress" around the top (*New York Public Library*)
(Right) Soldier of the Continental Army's Provisional Rifle Corps, wearing hunting shirt and blue leggings. He is armed with a "Kentucky" rifle. *Photo by Dr. Eric Nason, 2nd South Carolina Regiment.*

In addition to the above there were the 1ˢᵗ Continental Artillery Regiment, 2ⁿᵈ Continental Artillery Regiment and Virginia Continental Artillery Company plus two "extra" units that were under direct control of the Continental Congress:

- The Commander-in-Chief's Guard
- The Maryland and Virginia Rifle Regiment

The first one was also known as "Washington's Life Guard", was created on 11 March 1776 in order to act as the personal bodyguard for the Commander-in-Chief of the Continental Army and was under direct command of George Washington. It consisted of a single infantry company, which was also tasked with protecting the money and official papers of the Continental Army's general staff. Members of this elite corps were chosen in a peculiar way: each of the infantry regiments of the Continental Army, in fact, was required to send four of its best soldiers to create the new guard unit. The standard strength of the Commander-in-Chief's Guard was of 180 men, but these were augmented to 250 during the winter of 1779-1780. The corps included a small band with one drum-major, six drummers and six fifers.

Soldiers of the Provisional Rifle Corps at the Second Battle of Saratoga (October 1777).

The Maryland and Virginia Rifle Regiment was created in June 1776 by assembling three smaller independent corps of light infantry together: Rawlings' Independent Maryland Rifle Company, Williams' Independent Maryland Rifle Company and Stephenson's Independent Virginia Rifle Company. The new consolidated unit was a specialized corps having a distinct "ranger" character, which the soldiers were all equipped with excellent rifled muskets (differently from the soldiers of the line infantry, who mostly had smoothbore muskets). In total, the new Maryland and Virginia Rifle Regiment had nine companies: four were raised in Maryland and five were raised in Virginia. The riflemen of this elite unit soon proved to be a fundamental component of the Continental Army, thanks to their great combat capabilities. In November 1776, however, most of the regiment was captured by the British and thus the corps temporarily ceased to exist. In early 1777 a Provisional Rifle Corps, also known as Morgan's Riflemen from the name of its commander, was created to replace the Maryland and Virginia Rifle Regiment. This comprised just 500 soldiers in eight companies and ceased to exist in 1779, when the original Maryland and Virginia Rifle Regiment was re-raised. The re-formed unit (having just three companies) was mostly used to protect the western frontier of Pennsylvania from native raids and was finally disbanded in 1781.

Soldiers of the Continental Army. From left to right: infantryman of the Rhode Island Regiment of the Continental Line in summer dress (without coat), infantryman of the 2nd Canadian Regiment, soldier of the Provisional Rifle Corps and gunner of the Continental Artillery. The Rhode Island Regiment of the Continental Line did include a high percentage of black soldiers. (*NY Public Library*)

Continental regulars marching across a city. Popular support was one of the key factors behind the final success of the Continental Army, which logistical system worked well thanks to the support of many civilians.

Early in the war most of the Continental Army was made up of units recruited from the states of New England. The other states, in fact, contributed to the American war effort by recruiting military units that were not part of the Continental Army but served in five independent "departments": Canadian Department, Northern Department, Eastern Department, Middle Department and Southern Department. Each of the latter operated in an autonomous way against the British military forces. The order of battle of the five departments was:

Canadian Department

- Van Shaick's New York Regiment
- Nicholson's New York Regiment
- 5th New York Regiment
- 3rd Pennsylvania Regiment
- 5th Pennsylvania Regiment
- 7th Pennsylvania Regiment
- 1st Connecticut Regiment
- Burrall's Connecticut Regiment
- 2nd New Jersey Regiment
- Porter's Massachusetts Regiment
- Bedel's New Hampshire Regiment
- Warner's Vermont Regiment
- 1st Canadian Regiment
- 2nd Canadian Regiment

Northern Department

- 1st New York Regiment
- 2nd New York Regiment
- 4th New York Regiment
- 8th Pennsylvania Regiment
- 1st Pennsylvania Company of Artillery
- 1st New Jersey Regiment
- 3rd New Jersey Regiment
- 2nd Pennsylvania Regiment
- Elmore's Connecticut Regiment

Eastern Department

- Long's New Hampshire Regiment
- Ward's Connecticut Regiment
- Richmond's Rhode Island Regiment
- Babcock's Rhode Island Regiment

Middle Department

- 4th Pennsylvania Regiment
- 6th Pennsylvania Regiment
- Westmoreland Independent Companies
- 1st Maryland Regiment
- 2nd Maryland Regiment
- German Battalion
- Delaware Regiment

Southern Department

- 1st Virginia Regiment
- 2nd Virginia Regiment
- 3rd Virginia Regiment
- 4th Virginia Regiment
- 5th Virginia Regiment
- 6th Virginia Regiment
- 7th Virginia Regiment
- 8th Virginia Regiment
- 9th Virginia Regiment
- 1st South Carolina Regiment
- 2nd South Carolina Regiment
- 1st South Carolina Rifle Regiment
- 2nd South Carolina Rifle Regiment
- 1st North Carolina Regiment
- 2nd North Carolina Regiment
- 3rd North Carolina Regiment
- 4th North Carolina Regiment
- 5th North Carolina Regiment
- 6th North Carolina Regiment
- 1st Georgia Regiment
- North Carolina Light Dragoons Regiment
- Georgia Regiment of Horse Rangers
- South Carolina Artillery Regiment
- Virginia State Artillery Regiment

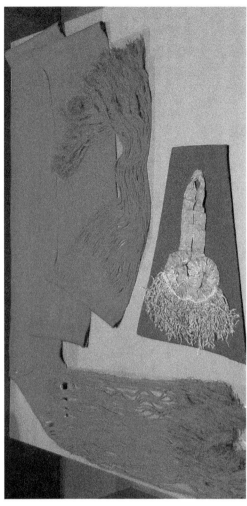

(Left) George Washington, Commander-in-Chief of the US military forces, wearing his famous "blue and buff" uniform. The latter was worn by all the officers of his General Staff as well as by those of the small Engineer Corps. (Right) An officer's sash and epaulette (Museum of the American Revolution).

All the units of the various departments listed above were "state troops" raised by the single colonies/states. Some of them had a quite peculiar history. The German Battalion of the Middle Department was initially raised from German settlers living in Maryland; later it became part of the Continental Army and was expanded up to nine companies (five formed in Pennsylvania and four in Maryland). The unit was disbanded in 1781. The two Westmoreland Independent Companies of the same department were organized to defend the frontier areas of Connecticut from native attacks and mostly performed garrison duties. The North Carolina Light Dragoons Regiment consisted of four companies and was disbanded in 1779; the Georgia Regiment of Horse Rangers, instead, initially consisted of four troops (later increased to 12) and was disbanded in 1781. The South Carolina Artillery Regiment initially comprised three companies (later increased to six) and was disbanded in 1781. As clear from the above list, each of the Thirteen Colonies had formed its own state troops by 1776 and these were separate entities from both the Continental Army and the militia. Maryland, Delaware, Virginia, North Carolina, South Carolina and Georgia had always been contrary to the creation of a common "American Army" and thus their contribution to the formation of the Continental military forces was quite scarce from a numerical point of view. They, instead, preferred to raise large numbers of state troops for the defence of their home territories.

Officers of the Continental Army in 1775. During the fist years of the war, many officers and soldiers continued to wear their civilian clothes and thus did not have a very "martial" appearance (H. Charles McBarron, Jr.).

The Consolidation of the Continental Army

In September 1776, when the second year of service of the Continental Army's units was about to expire, the Second Continental Congress decided to augment and re-organize the military forces at its command by passing the so-called "Eighty-eight Battalion Resolve". According to the latter, the new Continental Army would have comprised a total of 88 regiments provided by the single states according to the numerical consistency of their population. Since the great majority of the Continental infantry regiments consisted of a single battalion, the legislative act that re-structured the US military forces was known as "Eighty-eight Battalion Resolve" and not as "Eighty-eight Regiment Resolve". The military events of 1776 had clearly shown that the British had no intention to give up the fight and that they would have assembled large military forces in order to crush the American Revolution; as a result, the Second Continental Congress decided that the new units enlisted and organized for 1777 would have remained in service until the end of the hostilities with Great Britain. This way the Continental Army would have acquired a more consolidated and permanent character, which was absolutely fundamental for transforming it into a professional fighting force. George Washington could no longer command an army that had to be disbanded at the end of each year, since the war effort was reaching its peak. Each state was required to arm, clothe and equip a certain number of infantry regiments, which were collectively known as the "state's line". The new units organized in 1777 were raised from the various states as follows:

- Massachusetts: 15 regiments
- Virginia: 15 regiments
- Pennsylvania: 12 regiments
- North Carolina: 9 regiments
- Connecticut: 8 regiments
- South Carolina: 6 regiments
- Georgia: 1 regiment
- New York: 4 regiments
- New Jersey: 4 regiments
- New Hampshire: 3 regiments
- Rhode Island: 2 regiments
- Delaware: 1 regiment
- Maryland: 8 regiments

As clear from the above, the new structure of the Continental Army was quite different from the previous one: the five "territorial" departments were eliminated and also the southern states like Virginia had to contribute in a substantial way to the formation of the unified Continental military force. This was something particularly important, especially because since 1777 the military operations of the American Revolution started to be fought on a larger scale and to also involve the southern territories of the new country (where the presence of loyalists had always been very strong and still represented a serious menace). Washington and his generals, however, were not completely satisfied by this new establishment with 88 line infantry regiments; they were convinced, in fact, that more units were absolutely needed to face the British Army on almost equal terms. As a result, already in December 1776, the Congress gave to Washington the power to raise some "additional regiments" that would have been placed directly under his control and that would have been independent from the "line" establishments of the various states. The "additional regiments" of the Continental Army, raised at the beginning of 1777, were the following:

- **Forman's Additional Continental Regiment** (raised from New Jersey and Maryland, consolidated with Spencer's Additional Regiment in 1779)
- **Gist's Additional Continental Regiment** (raised from Virginia and Maryland, captured in May 1780)
- **Grayson's Additional Continental Regiment** (raised from Virginia, Maryland and Delaware; consolidated with Gist's Additional Regiment in 1779)
- **Hartley's Additional Continental Regiment** (raised in Pennsylvania, Maryland and Delaware; absorbed into the "Pennsylvania Line" in March 1778)
- **Henley's Additional Continental Regiment** (raised in Massachusetts, consolidated with Jackson's Additional Regiment in 1779)
- **Jackson's Additional Continental Regiment** (raised in Massachusetts, absorbed into the "Massachusetts Line" in July 1780)
- **Lee's Additional Continental Regiment** (raised in Massachusetts, consolidated with Jackson's Additional Regiment in 1779)
- **Malcolm's Additional Continental Regiment** (raised in New York and Pennsylvania, it was broken up during 1779 to reinforce some other infantry regiments lacking manpower)
- **Patton's Additional Continental Regiment** (raised in Pennsylvania, New Jersey and Delaware; consolidated with Hartley's Additional Regiment in 1779)
- **Sheppard's Additional Continental Regiment** (raised in North Carolina, disbanded in 1778)
- **Sherburne's Additional Continental Regiment** (raised in Rhode Island and Connecticut, disbanded in 1781)
- **Spencer's Additional Continental Regiment** (raised in New Jersey and Pennsylvania, disbanded in 1781)
- **Thruston's Additional Continental Regiment** (raised in Virginia, consolidated with Gist's Additional Regiment in 1779)
- **Webb's Additional Continental Regiment** (raised in Connecticut, absorbed into the "Connecticut Line" in July 1780)

Initially the "additional" infantry regiments authorized by Congress were 16, but only 14 were effectively raised. Most of these were formed by soldiers coming from different states and all of them were not numbered as the "standard" infantry units; they were, instead, named after their commanding colonel. On 27 May 1778, to cut economic costs, the number of "standard" infantry regiments in the Continental Army was reduced from 88 to 80 and a single company of light infantry was included in each unit (until then all the companies of an infantry regiment had been line ones). The number of companies in each unit was reduced from ten to nine. This was the new establishment resulting from the above modifications:

- Massachusetts: 15 regiments
- Virginia: 11 regiments
- Pennsylvania: 11 regiments
- North Carolina: 6 regiments
- Connecticut: 8 regiments
- South Carolina: 6 regiments
- Georgia: 1 regiment
- New York: 5 regiments
- New Jersey: 3 regiments
- New Hampshire: 3 regiments
- Rhode Island: 2 regiments
- Delaware: 1 regiment
- Maryland: 8 regiments

Continental Line 1777 - 1783

Private
2nd Maryland
1780

Private
5th Pennsylvania
1777-1783

Flag bearer
1st Rhode Island
1780

Private
1st Pennsylvania
1777-1780

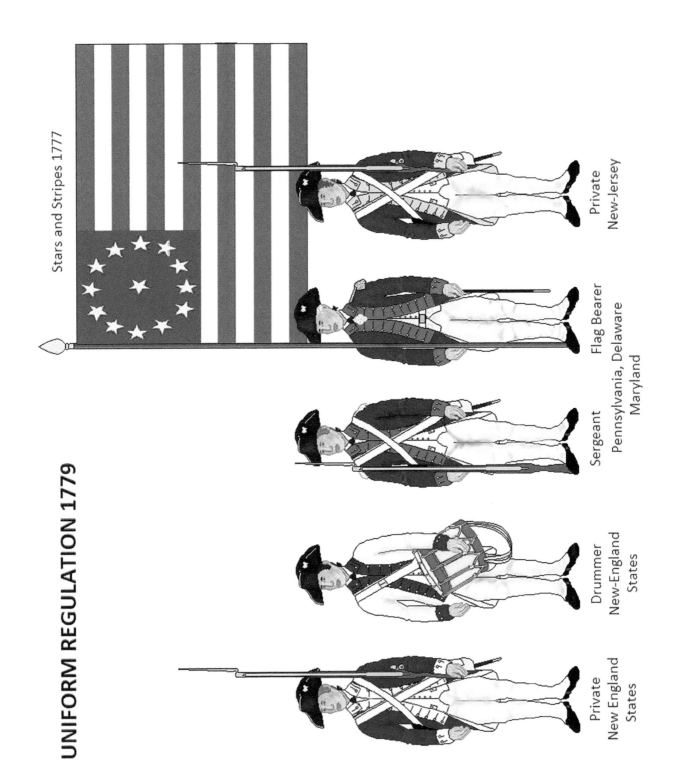

Stars and Stripes 1777

UNIFORM REGULATION 1779

Private
New-Jersey

Flag Bearer
Pennsylvania, Delaware
Maryland

Sergeant
Pennsylvania, Delaware
Maryland

Drummer
New-England
States

Private
New England
States

George Washington with two officers of his General Staff. The Commander-in-Chief had many difficulties in introducing European military tactics inside his Continental Army, but in the end he was able to reach his objective thanks to the help of several qualified officers coming from Europe (H. Charles McBarron, Jr.)

In March 1779 several of the existing "additional" regiments of infantry were consolidated into a smaller number of units, in order to have larger and better organized corps. In October 1780 the general structure of the Continental Army was modified again, with a general reduction in the number of line infantry regiments (which decreased from 80 to 49). These reductions were all caused by the need to cut military budgets and by the requests of the single states, many of which (especially in the south) had no intention to spend large sums of money to finance Washington's army until the end of the hostilities with Great Britain. According to these states' view, in fact, the war could be fought with just a small number of regular units supplemented by the state militias and thus there was no need to expand the Continental Army over 50 infantry regiments. This was the general establishment resulting from the new cuts:

- Massachusetts: 10 regiments
- Virginia: 8 regiments
- Pennsylvania: 6 regiments
- North Carolina: 4 regiments
- Connecticut: 5 regiments
- South Carolina: 2 regiments
- Georgia: 1 regiment

-New York: 2 regiments
-New Jersey: 2 regiments
-New Hampshire: 2 regiments
-Rhode Island: 1 regiment
-Delaware: 1 regiment
Maryland: 5 regiments

The Commander-in-Chief and some of the officers from his General Staff (including an artillery one, with red facings, on the right). On campaign, especially during winter, the frontal lapels of the coat were frequently worn buttoned-up.

The remaining "additional" regiments were also affected by reorganization of 1780: they were absorbed into the "line" of the single states or were simply disbanded. After the Siege of Yorktown, with the final expulsion of the British troops from US soil, the Continental Army was re-structured for a last time on 7 August 1782. Many of the existing "line" regiments were disbanded or adopted a new establishment with less than nine companies (thus becoming battalions). Each of the states was to provide the following corps, according to a reduced general structure that was maintained until the end of the hostilities in 1783:

- Massachusetts: 8 regiments
- Virginia: 2 regiments
- Pennsylvania: 3 regiments
- North Carolina: 1 regiment and 1 battalion
- Connecticut: 3 regiments
- South Carolina: 2 regiments
- Georgia: 1 battalion

- New York: 2 regiments
- New Jersey: 1 regiment and 1 battalion
- New Hampshire: 1 regiment and 1 battalion
- Rhode Island: 1 battalion
- Delaware: 1 battalion
- Maryland: 2 regiments

It should be remembered, however, that during the period 1777-1783 the Continental Army continued to comprise some "extra" units that were under direct control of the Congress. These have already been analysed before and consisted of the following corps:

- Commander-in-Chief's Guard
- 1st Canadian Regiment (disbanded in 1781)
- 2nd Canadian Regiment (disbanded in 1783)
- Elmore's Regiment (disbanded in 1777)
- Maryland and Virginia Rifle Regiment (disbanded in 1781)
- Westmoreland Independent Companies (disbanded in 1781)

- Ward's Regiment (disbanded in 1777)
- New Hampshire Rangers (disbanded in 1781)
- German Battalion (disbanded in 1781)
- Long's Regiment (disbanded in 1777)

(Left) Soldiers from a light infantry company of a line regiment. They are wearing the new uniform prescribed in 1779 and the peculiar light infantry cap of their regiment (in this case a "Tarleton" helmet). (right top) South Carolina light infantry cap. (Right bottom) Newport Light Infantry cap (American Revolution Museum).

The Jersey Blues as scouts in the American Revolution, 1783. *Theopile Lybaert, 1904.*

"The Smoker" a drummer of the New Jersey Blues.
Theopile Lybaert

To conclude this section dedicated to the Continental Army, we must provide some details on a little-known "temporary" combat force that was organized during the Siege of Yorktown: the so-called "Light Infantry Division". The latter was created on 24 September 1781 by assembling together several light units of the Continental Army, in order to form a special force of lightly-equipped "assault troops" that could storm the British fortifications of Yorktown. Command of this special division was given to the Marquis de Lafayette, one of Washington's greatest generals and probably the most famous foreign officer of the Continental Army. Basically the Light Infantry Division was created by assembling together the light companies of several line infantry regiments, which were detached from their "mother" units, much like the European habit of amalgamating grenadier companies into consolidated battalions. The new division commanded by Lafayette was structured on two brigades with three units each, most of the latter being "temporary" corps made up of companies coming from different regiments. The Light Infantry Division fought with great courage during the Siege of Yorktown and was one of the key factors that determined the final victory of the Continental Army. The general quality of its soldiers was particularly high, since members of the light infantry companies were usually selected because of their superior personal capabilities. This was the order of battle of the division:

1st Brigade

- **Vose's Battalion**, consisting of the light infantry companies from the regiments of Massachusetts Line numbered 1-8
- **Gimat's Battalion**, consisting of the light infantry companies from the regiments of Massachusetts Line numbered 9-10 as well as from those of the 2nd Rhode Island Regiment of the Line and 1st-5th Connecticut Regiments of the Line
- **Barber's Battalion**, consisting of the light infantry companies from the 1st-2nd New Hampshire Regiments of the Line as well as from those of the 1st-5th New Jersey Regiments of the Line

2nd Brigade

- **Canadian Regiment** (previously known as 2nd Canadian Regiment)
- **Scammell's Light Infantry Regiment**, formed by eight temporary light infantry companies that were created by selecting the best infantrymen who served in the line units. Three companies were raised from regiments of the Massachusetts Line, three from regiments of the Connecticut Line and two from regiments of the New Hampshire Line
- **Hamilton's Battalion**, consisting of the light infantry companies from the 1st-2nd New York Regiments of the Line as well as from two temporary light infantry companies that were created by selecting the best infantrymen who served in the Connecticut Line

The formation of the Light Infantry Division, from a tactical point of view, was not something completely new: during the previous years of war, in fact, the light companies of the line regiments had been often detached from their "mother" units in order to form some special "temporary" battalions. During the campaign that culminated with the Battle of Saratoga in 1777, for example, a provisional

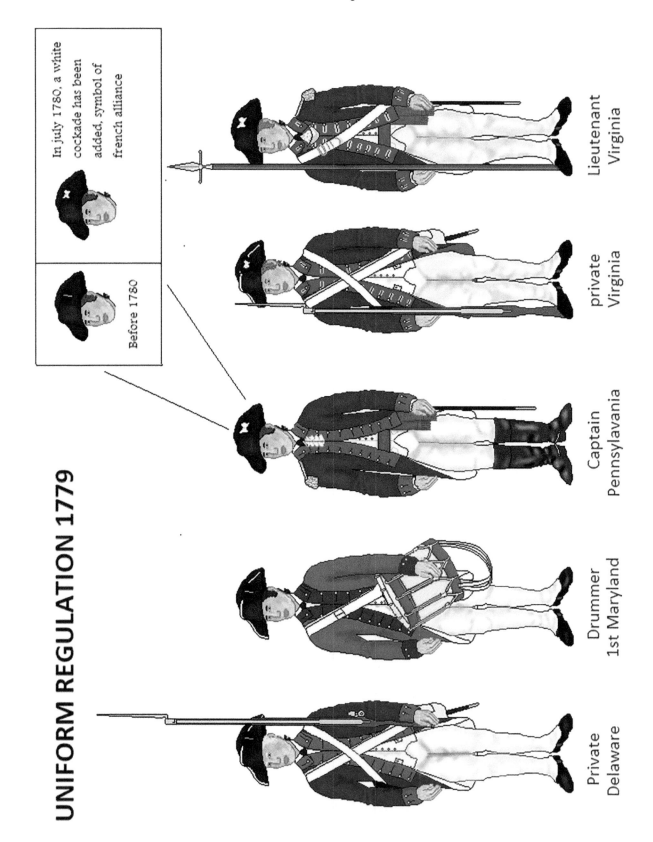

UNIFORM REGULATION 1779

In july 1780, a white cockade has been added, symbol of french alliance

Before 1780

Lieutenant Virginia

private Virginia

Captain Pennsylavania

Drummer 1st Maryland

Private Delaware

"Light Infantry Regiment" under command of Henry Dearborn had already been organized. It should be noted, however, that the creation of the Light Infantry Division was the largest of such "experiments" and that it obtained significant results. The soldiers of the six temporary units that made up the division retained the uniforms of their original regiments, but their commander Lafayette ordered them to add some black and red plumes on their headgear as a mark of distinction.

Soldier from the light infantry company of the 2nd South Carolina Regiment of the Continental Line. The green "epaulette" on the right shoulder was distinctive of light infantrymen. *Photo by Dr. Eric Nason, 2nd South Carolina Regiment.*

To sum up, we could divide the history of the Continental Army into four main phases: the first, corresponding to the year 1775, saw the formation of the new "unified" military force by raising regiments that mostly came from New England; the second, corresponding to the year 1776, saw the expansion of the Continental forces and the creation of five "territorial" departments that were independent from Washington's direct command; the third, corresponding to the years 1777-1779, saw the maximum expansion and consolidation of the Continental Army; the fourth, corresponding to the years 1780-1783, saw the gradual demobilization of the forces that had defeated the British. During all these phases the Continental infantry continued to comprise three main categories of troops: "line" regiments provided by the various states according to their population, which made up the bulk of the Continental military forces; "extra" regiments, having specific tasks or being recruited from foreigners, which were under direct control of the Congress; "additional" regiments, made up of soldiers coming from different states, which were under direct control of George Washington. In

Left: Soldiers of the Continental Army, wearing M1779 uniforms. The two on the left are infantrymen from the southern states (the Carolinas or Georgia) as shown by the dark blue facings of their coats; the one on the right is an artilleryman, having dark blue coat with red facings.

Right: Continental infantryman, wearing pre-1779 dress. Black tricorn and dark blue coat with red facings were the most common combination that could be found in Continental uniforms before 1779. Soft caps like that worn by the figure on the right were a popular alternative to the tricorn on campaign.

1775, soon after its creation, the Continental Army was not so different from the state militias in terms of training and discipline: it was only thanks to Washington's great efforts, in fact, that it gradually developed a distinct identity and learned how to fight by using conventional tactics. The hit-and-run attacks of the minutemen worked well when small contingents of British soldiers had to be ambushed, but were of little use when large, pitched battles had to be fought. Changing the mentality of an entire military force was not something simple and thus Washington had to face a strong internal opposition coming from his own subordinates; the Commander-in-Chief, however, acted in a very intelligent way and was able to improve the general quality of his Continentals thanks to the precious collaboration of some expert officers coming from Europe. These re-trained the Continental Army according to contemporary European practices and improved a lot the discipline of the troops under their command.

The Continental line infantry at the Battle of Guilford Court House (March 15, 1781). As clear from this picture, also after the introduction of the 1779 dress regulations many of the American soldiers continued to wear hunting shirts instead of their "regular" coats. In this case the unit depicted is the 1st Maryland Regiment of the Continental Line.

During the winter of 1777-1778, at the Valley Forge Camp, the Prussian Baron von Steuben completely re-trained the infantry of the Continental Army; thanks to his great experience as an officer in the Prussian Army of Frederick the Great, at that time the best military force of the world, he was appointed as Inspector General of the Continental Army by George Washington. The Baron improved a lot the administrative structures of the army and established new rules dealing with the construction of camps. Order and discipline were the key elements behind the success of any fighting force, and these had to be found in every aspect of a soldier's daily life. After these first improvements, the Baron decided to re-train Washington's Life Guard according to contemporary Prussian practices in order to transform it into a "model unit" for the rest of the Continental Army. Washington was particularly impressed by the demonstrations made by the Prussian officers with the Life Guard and thus ordered him to use the same training system for all Continentals. It was during this crucial period that Baron von Steuben wrote the "Regulations for the Order and Discipline of the Troops of the United States", the first drill manual in the history of the US military. The latter prescribed a system of "progressive training", beginning with the single soldier and ending at regimental level. The Prussian officer also introduced significant tactical innovations, for example in the use of the bayonet: until his reforms, in fact, American infantrymen had never been able to launch frontal bayonet charges and always used their muskets only to fire from a certain distance. Baron von Steuben, however, was not the only foreign officer who played a crucial role in improving the general quality of the Continental Army; in this sense we have already remembered the contribution given by Lafayette for light infantry and we will analyse the role played by some other important officers (Pulaski for cavalry and Duportail for engineers).

A depiction of an American general and rifleman from an English engraving (New York Public Library)

After the end of the American Revolution, the great Continental Army created and forged under George Washington was disbanded by the Congress. The Treaty of Paris, bringing the war between Great Britain and the USA to an end, was signed on 3 September 1783: by that time the American Army was camped along the Hudson River at New Windsor, after having terminated the siege operations against Yorktown. It comprised approximately 7,000/8,000 men, all veterans who had served their young nation with great courage. By the end of the war, however, many of these soldiers were ill-clad and underfed: they lacked adequate supplies and had not been paid for a long time. The difficulties of a terrible war had caused serious problems to the economy of the new nation and the USA was no longer in condition nor had the desire to maintain a large military force of regulars. With the defeat of the British, it was now time to demobilize the Continental Army and thus cut the military costs in a significant way. On 24 September 1783, shortly after the signing of the Paris Treaty, the Congress formally ordered Washington to demobilize the Continental Army. The demobilization order was not too strict: the Commander-in-Chief, in fact, was free to decide how many soldiers should remain under arms. The great general waited for some time, until the last British troops abandoned New York, before reorganizing the US Army. According to the new structure in place since late 1783, the latter was to be an amalgamation of just 600 men organized into one regiment of infantry with two attached companies of artillery. The senior artillery company came from "Lamb's Continental Artillery Regiment"; the junior one was raised in Pennsylvania. The new infantry unit was known as "1st American Regiment" or as "Jackson's Continental Regiment" since it was commanded by Colonel Henry Jackson. From a formal point of view, the Continental Army was not disbanded but now condensed to this single unit (this being the reason why the latter had the adjective "Continental" in its name). This corps lasted until 3 June 1784: on that date a new "1st American Regiment" was formally established,

which was theoretically organized on nine companies; during those same days, all the other units of the Continental Army were disbanded. Most of the soldiers who made up the new regiment were veterans coming from the Massachusetts "line". Obviously 500 infantrymen and 100 artillerymen were not enough to defend the boundaries of the new nation, but the Congress and the majority of the Americans, at least for the moment, were not in favour of maintaining a large permanent force.

NCO (left) and soldiers (right) from four different infantry regiments of the Continental Army, with pre-1779 dress. Each unit had facings in a distinctive colour; buttonholes, as visible here, could be decorated with additional lace in a contrasting colour.

Continental soldiers wearing their new M1779 dress. The figure on the left is an artilleryman, the one on the right is a NCO from an infantry regiment recruited in New York or New Jersey (as clear from the buff colour of the facings). The red facings of the artillery regiments could be decorated with additional yellow piping and lace on the buttonholes, but on campaign it was not common to see such decorations.

Alexander Hamilton at the lines of Yorktown in the uniform of the New York Artillery. *Alonzo Cheppel.*

The cut of a uniform coat, breeches and vest from the revolutionary era. *NYPL*

Cavalry, technical corps, partisan units and Marines

Until the general reorganization of 1777, the Continental Army mostly remained a line infantry force. Washington and his generals, however, had understood since the beginning of the hostilities that some effective units of cavalry and artillery were necessary if the Continental military forces wanted to face their British opponents on equal terms. Cavalry was necessary to conduct reconnaissance operations, while artillery was fundamental during siege operations and field battles. The Continental cavalry started to be organized around March 1777; it was to consist of four regiments of light dragoons, each having 280 soldiers in six troops. Overall command of the Continental Light Dragoons was given to Count Casimir Pulaski, a Polish nobleman who is still known today as the "Father of the American Cavalry". Pulaski came from an important Polish family having a glorious military past and served as a leading commander for the military forces of the Bar Confederation during the Polish civil conflict known as "War of the Bar Confederation" (1768-1772). After the Polish patriots of the Bar Confederation were defeated by the Russian Army, he left Poland for France where he was persuaded by Benjamin Franklin to go to North America along with Michael Kovats where they joined the local revolutionaries in their struggle against the British colonial government. Pulaski was an experienced cavalry commander and a great tactician; after assuming control of the newly formed Continental cavalry, he soon understood that the latter would have been employed not as a "shock" force tasked with conducting frontal charges but as a reconnaissance/scouting force made up of mounted scouts. As a result, the four regiments that made up the US mounted forces were

The banner of Pulaski's Legion (New York Public Library)

equipped and trained since the beginning as light dragoons; their members learned to move rapidly on every kind of terrain and were also drilled to fight as infantrymen when needed. On 28 March 1778, due to personal frictions with some of his subordinate commanders, Pulaski resigned from command of the Continental Light Dragoons and decided to form an independent military unit (known as Pulaski's Legion, see below for more details). After this event the four mounted regiments, which had been assembled into a single cavalry brigade, were despatched to different geographical areas and started to operate into smaller troop-sized detachments. During 1778 the formal establishment of each cavalry regiment was increased to 415 troopers, but this number was never reached by any of the four units; it should be remembered, in addition, that only a certain number of soldiers in each troop were effectively mounted (since there were too few horses). Transforming the light dragoons from a cavalry brigade to a series of small scouting detachments had been a clear mistake from a tactical point of view, since the Continental horsemen were of limited use when employed in small numbers on vast fronts.

In January 1781, following a contemporary European practice, the four regiments of light dragoons were transformed into four "legions": the latter were "mixed" units comprising infantry and cavalry, having great tactical flexibility and being trained as light troops. Each of the new "legions" was to comprise four troops of horse ~~troops~~ and two infantry companies; in addition, each of the light dragoon units was assigned to a state: the 1st and 3rd to Virginia, the 2nd to Connecticut and the 4th to Pennsylvania. During 1782, the two mounted corps assigned to Virginia were consolidated into a single unit. This was the order of battle of the Continental cavalry during the American Revolution:

- 1st Continental Light Dragoons, also known as "Bland's Horse", 1st Legionary Corps, 1781
- 2nd Continental Light Dragoons, also known as "Sheldon's Horse", 2nd Legionary Corps, 1781
- 3rd Continental Light Dragoons, also known as "Baylor's Horse", 3rd Legionary Corps, 1781
- 4th Continental Light Dragoons, also known as "Moylan's Horse", 4th Legionary Corps, 1781

Continental Light Dragoons. Those with white coats on the left are from the 3rd Regiment, while those with dark blue coats on the right are from the 2nd Regiment. *Photo by Dr. Eric Nason, 2nd South Carolina Regiment.*

CAVALRY 1777 - 1783

Trooper
4th Light Dragoon
1779-1782

Officer
3rd Light Dragoon
1778-1779

Trooper
3rd Light Dragoon
1779

Trooper
2nd Light Dragoon
1780-1783

Trumpeter
1st Light Dragoon
1777

Trooper
1st Light Dragoon
1777

The first unit had originally been formed as part of Virginia's "state troops", on six troops, with the denomination of Virginia Light Horse Regiment. After the corps was absorbed into the Continental Army, its internal structure was expanded and changed. The regimental staff consisted of the following elements: one colonel, one lieutenant-colonel, one major, one chaplain, one quartermaster, one surgeon, one assistant-surgeon, one paymaster, one riding master, one saddler, one trumpet-major, one adjutant and four cadets. Each troop was made up of the following elements: one captain, one lieutenant, one cornet, one drill sergeant, one quartermaster sergeant, four corporals, one trumpeter, one farrier, one armourer and 32 troopers. The 5th Troop of the 1st Continental Light Dragoons was commanded by Captain Henry "Light Horse Harry" Lee, father of Robert Edward Lee, who was a great expert of light cavalry tactics. In April 1778 it was detached from its original "mother" unit in order to be transformed into an independent corps known as "Lee's Legion" (see below for more details); as a result, a new troop had to be raised in order to substitute the one commanded by Captain Henry Lee. During most of the American Revolution, the four Continental cavalry units described above were supported by two mounted regiments that were not part of the Continental Army but that were attached to it: the North Carolina Light Dragoons and the Georgia Regiment of Horse Rangers, which we have already analysed before. These two units were "state troops" from North Carolina and Georgia but had the same standards of service of the Continental Light Dragoons.

Trooper of the Virginia Light Dragoons, with the uniform used by this unit before becoming the 1st Regiment of Continental Light Dragoons. *Photo by the 1st Virginia Regiment of the Continental Line.*

(Left) Lee's Legion in the field

(below) Examples of cavalry sabres from the 1770's.

ARTILLERY

With the reorganization of 1777 the artillery of the Continental Army was expanded and re-structured on four regiments, which were assembled together into a single brigade commanded by Henry Knox. This was the order of battle of the Continental artillery during the American Revolution:

- 1st Continental Artillery Regiment, also known as "Harrison's Regiment"
- 2nd Continental Artillery Regiment, also known as "Lamb's Regiment"
- 3rd Continental Artillery Regiment, also known as "Crane's Regiment"
- 4th Continental Artillery Regiment, also known as "Proctor's Regiment"

Continental artillerymen, with the new uniform introduced since 1779.

The first unit was raised in Virginia as the Continental Artillery Regiment, with ten companies/batteries. Two of the latter were initially formed as part of Virginia's "state troops". During May 1780, after absorbing three independent artillery companies raised in Maryland, the regiment was increased to 12 batteries; in 1781 it was reduced to 10 companies before being finally disbanded in 1783. Each of this regiment's companies/batteries comprised the following elements: four officers, one sergeant, four corporals, four bombardiers, eight gunners and 48 matrosses. In August 1779, like all other artillery regiments, this corps received a progressive number. Like "Harrison's Regiment", as well as "Lamb's Regiment" which existed prior to 1777; as anticipated above, it comprised a total of 12 companies/batteries: six from New York, four from Connecticut and two from Pennsylvania. Three of the six companies from New York already existed before 1776 as independent "state" artillery companies. In 1781 the regiment was reduced to ten companies and then to two in 1783. The 3rd Continental Artillery Regiment was organized in January 1777 and had an initial establishment of 12 companies/batteries, recruited from Massachusetts and Rhode Island.

For a certain period of time, three of the latter were detached from their "mother" unit in order to form an independent corps known as "Stevens' Provisional Artillery Battalion" (which was disbanded at the end of 1778). In January 1781 the number of companies was reduced from 12 to 10; during 1783 the latter were reduced to 4 before the regiment was disbanded in 1784. The 4th Artillery Regiment became part of the Continental Army during 1777 but it was originally formed as an artillery battalion with two companies that was part of Pennsylvania "state troops". This Pennsylvania State Artillery Battalion was later transformed into a regiment with 8 companies/batteries at the beginning of 1777. Four of the new companies were obtained by absorbing into the corps a new artillery regiment that had been created as part of Pennsylvania's "state troops". Each of the 8 companies was to comprise the following elements: one captain, one captain-lieutenant, one first-lieutenant, two second-lieutenants, six sergeants, six corporals, six bombardiers, six gunners and 28 matrosses. In January 1781 the 4th Continental Artillery Regiment was expanded to 10 companies/batteries, before being reduced to just four companies in January 1783 (the corps was finally disbanded some months later, on 15 November 1783). Since the beginning of 1781, like the cavalry regiments, also the artillery ones were assigned to some states: Virginia for the 1st Artillery, New York for the 2nd Artillery, Massachusetts for the 3rd Artillery and Pennsylvania for the 4th Artillery.

The 2nd Continental Artillery Regiment, also known as "Lamb's Continental Artillery Regiment" from the name of its commander, comprised a total of 12 companies/batteries: six from New York, four from Connecticut and two from Pennsylvania. Three of the six companies from New York already existed before 1776 as independent "state" artillery companies. In 1781 Lamb's Regiment was reduced to ten companies and then to two in 1783.

Continental artillerymen with a 3-pound cannon. *Photo by Dr. Eric Nason, 2nd South Carolina Regiment.*

Continental artillerymen firing a 6-pound cannon. *Photo by Dr. Eric Nason, 2ⁿᵈ South Carolina Regiment.*

Continental artillerymen with a 6-pound cannon. *Photo by Dr. Eric Nason, 2ⁿᵈ South Carolina Regiment.*

Continental 3-pound cannon. *Photo by Dr. Eric Nason, 2nd South Carolina Regiment.*

Continental 12-pound howitzer. *Photo by Dr. Eric Nason, 2nd South Carolina Regiment.*

Continental artillery park. *Photo by Dr. Eric Nason, 2nd South Carolina Regiment.*

At the beginning of the war there was limited access to artillery pieces or their casting. Initially there were some militia units with artillery from pre-war companies, then the army acquired British guns and eventually French pieces. In theory, the companies were organized in British fashion with six-pieces (5 guns and one howitzer). Except for sieges, field pieces tended to be lighter to ease movement, but units used what they had available to them. Artillery was moved by limber or wagons, sometime relying on civilian contractors to move them.

In addition to the artillery, the Continental Army did comprise also some other "technical corps" that had small establishments: the Engineer Corps, the Sappers and Miners Corps and the Artillery Artificer Regiment. At the beginning of the American Revolution, there were just a few military officers with solid engineering skills in the Thirteen Colonies; as a result, George Washington had great difficulties in organizing an effective staff of engineers who could help him during siege operations. The latter became increasingly frequent with the expansion of the war and thus the need for an effective Engineer Corps started to be felt in the Continental Army. Luckily, with the progression of time, an increasing number of expert officers having the needed competences came at the disposal of Washington: these were all European volunteers or exiles, who had served in the military forces of their respective countries before joining the American cause. One of these, the French Louis Duportail,

Louis Duportail (1743 - 1802). (*Wikipedia*)

was soon chosen as the commander of the new Engineer Corps that was in the process of being organized. Duportail demonstrated to have great organizational skills and was able to set up a small but effective staff of engineer officers. Another of these was Thaddeus Kosciuszko, who was commissioned a Colonel of the Engineers in 1776. Koscisuzko, like Lafayette, would go on to lead revolutions in his native country.

The Engineer Corps of the Continental Army always remained a very small unit, having a semi-permanent status: it consisted of just a few officers (most of whom were foreigners) who were tasked with building new fortifications and with directing siege operations. With the progression of time these expert engineers improved a lot the technical capabilities of the Continental Army, as shown by the successes obtained during the Siege of Yorktown in 1781. Duportail is still remembered today as one the "father" of the US Engineer Corps. Kosciuszko would go on to design the Fortification at West Point, the Saratoga Campaign and the Southern Campaign in 1780.

The Sappers and Miners Corps consisted of just three companies that were raised in May 1778, at the insistence of Louis Duportail. Its main duty was that of acting as the "labour force" of the Engineer Corps. Members of this unit, in fact, could perform as sappers or as miners: the first were combat engineers, trained to build field fortifications during pitched battles; the second were employed during siege operations, in order to perform mining and counter-mining. Sappers

also had to clear obstacles in the path of the army when the latter was advancing and could build infrastructures like bridges; they also had to establish camps when needed. The activities of the miners, mining and counter-mining, were particularly dangerous: a mine was a tunnel dug under the walls of an enemy fortification and then either set on fire or exploded in order to cause the collapse of the besieged fortified position. Counter-mining was the exact opposite of mining: it consisted of digging tunnels from a besieged fortress in order to intercept and destroy the mines that had been built by the besiegers. Under direction of the Engineer Corps' officers, the three companies of Sappers and Miners performed extremely well during the last phase of the American Revolution and especially at the Siege of Yorktown. Each of them comprised the following elements: four officers, eight NCOs and 60 soldiers; when building field fortifications or conducting mining operations, however, they could be supplemented by "temporary" drafts taken from the line infantry regiments that were put at the orders of the Engineer Corps.

Tadeusz Kosciuszko (1746 - 1817) (*Wikipedia*)

The Artillery Artificer Regiment was formed in February 1778 and was commanded by Colonel Benjamin Flower. It performed a series of duties that were essential for the correct functioning of

Camp of the Continental Army with white tents and field artillery pieces. *Photo by Dr. Eric Nason, 2nd South Carolina Regiment.*

the artillery, like constructing and repairing gun carriages or limbers. The unit was also responsible for some important logistical functions, like providing the needed ammunition to the various field batteries. In July 1778 a new unit of artificers, known as Quartermaster's Artificer Regiment, was created to supplement the existing one; during 1781, however, the latter was absorbed into the Artillery Artificer Regiment.

In addition to the three technical corps described above, the Continental Army also had another two small units that performed "auxiliary" duties: the Provost Corps and the Invalid Corps. The first was a unit of military police, consisting of a single mounted troop which components were equipped like light dragoons. Members of this corps were mostly German colonists who were trained to act as "gendarmes"; their duties included rounding up deserters and hanging offenders. In practice, the Provost Corps had as primary function of enforcing military law and discipline in the Continental Army, by supporting the Judge Advocate General in his activities. The military police unit, raised in 1778, was extremely efficient and also acted as the mounted escort for Washington's general staff. It comprised the following elements: one captain, four lieutenants, two trumpeters, two sergeants, four corporals, one clerk, one quartermaster sergeant, four executioners and 43 provosts. The Invalid Corps was made up of veteran soldiers who had been wounded in combat and who were no longer fit for active service; these individuals, however, could still be employed to perform "static" duties like garrison service. They were mostly tasked with guarding prisoners and garrisoning fortifications. The

Artillery

Captain
Continental Art
1781

Matross 2Nd
Continental Art
1781

Drummer
Continental Art
1779 Regulation

Gunner
Continental Art
1779 Regulation

Gunner
Knox's Artillery
regiment
1776

Continental Legions

Officer
Armand's Legion

Private
Pulaski's Legion
1779

Officer
Lee's Legion

Private
Lee's Legion

Invalid Corps was formed in June 1777 and initially it was designed to act also as a "training unit" for NCOs (something that never happened).

The Continental Army also contained three "Partisan Corps", which were highly specialized combat units trained to perform guerrilla and counter-guerrilla warfare by using unconventional methods. The Partisan Corps were mixed units of infantry and cavalry, which members all had light personal equipment; one of their main tasks was that of contrasting the activities of the Loyalists, who supported the British Army by organizing raids against the most isolated settlements (sometimes with the help of their native allies). The Partisan Corps of the Continental Army had small establishment if compared to the other units but were much more flexible than the latter: for example, they could be easily broken up to serve in many detachments. They were four in total, named after their commanders: Armand's Legion, Ottendorf's Corps, Pulaski's Legion and Lee's Legion. The term "legion" was used because these corps comprised both infantry and cavalry elements. Armand's Legion was formed in June 1778 at Boston, from foreign volunteers who were in Massachusetts. The latter were mostly French, like the same Colonel Charles Armand Tuffin who commanded the legion; this was a very experienced officer, who had served in the French Army as part of the "Garde du Corps" (i.e. the mounted bodyguard of the French monarch). Armand had left his country after injuring his king's cousin during a duel; after reaching North America, he soon joined the cause of the local revolutionaries. With the progression of time, due to the heavy losses suffered, the Armand's Legion had to recruit foreign prisoners of war (mostly Germans) in order to keep its original establishment; the general quality of the unit, however, did not decrease in a significant way. In 1780 it absorbed the remnants of Pulaski's Legion, which had been recently disbanded; during 1781 it was re-named as the 1st Partisan Corps of the Continental Army. Initially Armand's Legion had the designation of "Free and Independent Chasseurs" and consisted of just three companies; very soon, however, it changed name and was expanded to four companies. After absorbing the remnants of Pulaski's Legion, the unit received another company. Until 1781 it consisted only of light infantry; after assuming the new designation of 1st Partisan Corps, however, it was reorganized with three companies of light infantry and three troops of light dragoons. The Ottendorf's Corps was the most short-lived of the Partisan Corps included in the Continental Army. It was organized during December 1776 in eastern Pennsylvania and was mostly made up of German colonists, who were at the orders of Nicholas Dietrich (Baron of Ottendorf). The unit comprised 150 soldiers who were organized into three companies of light infantry and two companies of riflemen. In April 1778 the corps was disbanded and one of its companies was absorbed into Armand's Legion.

Pulaski's Legion was created on 28 March 1778 at Baltimore, in Maryland. It consisted of one troop of lancers, two troops of light dragoons and two companies of light infantry. Pulaski's lancers were the only horsemen of the Continental Army who were not equipped as standard light cavalry; they were, in fact, trained to operate as the "uhlans" (i.e. lancers) of the contemporary Polish Army. A high percentage of the soldiers in Pulaski's Legion were Polish exiles, who had abandoned their homeland after the fall of the Bar Confederation. This partisan unit fought with distinction on several occasions and suffered very severe losses soon after its formation; it was disbanded in November 1780 due to excessive casualties and its surviving members were absorbed into Armand's Legion. Lee's Legion was organized as an independent unit on 7 April 1778; until that moment, in fact, it had been one of the troops in the 1st Regiment of Light Dragoons (raised in Virginia). The new unit mostly served in the southern states, where it was employed with great success against the local Loyalists. It was the American equivalent of the famous Tarleton's Raiders, a unit of Loyalists that was uniformed in green with light dragoon helmets exactly like Lee's Legion. The latter soon gained a reputation for efficiency, bravery and ruthlessness that was unrivalled in the Continental Army. The commander of the legion, Henry Lee, was a real master in organizing ambushes and did know how to employ hit-and-run tactics in a very effective way. Initially Lee's Legion consisted of just three companies, which members could act both as light dragoons and light infantrymen; during July 1779 it was expanded to four companies, after absorbing a small "independent" partisan corps from Delaware. In January 1781 it assumed the new denomination of 2nd Partisan Corps, being reorganized on three companies of light dragoons and three companies of light infantrymen. By the end of the American Revolution, only two Partisan units remained in the Continental Army: the 1st Partisan Corps (mostly made up of foreign volunteers) and the 2nd Partisan Corps (mostly made up of volunteers coming from Virginia and the Carolinas). Both units were disbanded at the end of the war together with the rest of Washington's army.

Soon after the beginning of the hostilities with Great Britain, the Second Continental Congress had to organize some sort of "American Navy" in order to counter the power of the Royal Navy. On 10 November 1775, one month after the naval forces had been created, a "Continental Marine Act" was promulgated by the Congress according to which the new Continental Navy was to comprise two battalions of Marines (naval infantry). The latter would have been raised from good seamen, all having sailing experience and solid personal reputation. Each battalion of Marines was to comprise one colonel, two lieutenant-colonels and two majors plus a variable number of NCOs and privates. The Continental Marines were tasked with providing armed support to the sailors of the American warships; in addition, they had to defend the vessels and installations of the Navy and were also trained to form landing parties in order to conduct amphibious operations. In practice, the Marines were a multi-tasking elite corps since their foundation. Initially just one battalion with five companies could be organized; it was raised in the famous Tun's Tavern of Philadelphia by "drumming up" recruits from the streets of the city. The second battalion was organized, always on five companies, only at a later time. Soon after their creation, the Continental Marines were shown to be highly disciplined and well trained: for example, they carried out with success some amphibious landings and raids against the British colonies in the West Indies (during which substantial quantities of naval supplies were captured from the enemy). Usually, the companies that made up a battalion were detached

Soldiers of the Continental Army. The infantryman with dark brown coat having white facings is from the 1st Canadian Regiment, the soldier with red waistcoat is from the Commander-in-Chief's Guard, the man with light dragoon uniform is from the Provost Corps and the soldier with white hunting shirt is from the Provisional Rifle Corps.

to serve on board of the various warships, but sometimes several of them could be grouped together in order to operate as land troops (as it happened in 1777). During naval battles the Marines fought as sharpshooters and were mostly tasked with killing enemy officers and sailors; during boarding operations, they could mount bayonet assaults and capture enemy ships after some hand-to-hand combat. If needed, they could also man the guns of the warships on which they were serving; in addition, they kept order among the crew as a sort of "naval police" (mutinies were quite frequent). In April 1783, after having served with great distinction, the Continental Marines were disbanded; they would have been re-formed as the "US Marines" only during 1798.

Militia and State Troops

During the American Revolution, despite the creation of the Continental Army, each state continued to have its own militia and "state" troops. Generally, militia were used within a state, while "state" troops were assigned to serve in the Continental army. The militia supported George Washington's military forces on several occasions during the hostilities, but they always showed their usual limits: they could be employed only for short periods of service and could be of some use only when defending their home territories. State troops usually had better organization and training than militia units, since they were semi-permanent and semi-regular corps like the Provincials of the French and Indian War. This is a detailed list of all the militia units and state troops that were active on the territory of the Thirteen Colonies during the American Revolution:

Connecticut

1st Company Governor's Foot Guard, 1771
2nd Company Governor's Foot Guard, 1775
1st Company Governor's Horse Guard,1778

1st Battalion State Regiment, 1776–77
1st Regiment of Militia, 1778–79
2nd Regiment of Militia, 1776
3rd Regiment of Foot, 1775
3rd Regiment of Militia, 1776
4th Regiment of Militia, 1775–76
5th Regiment of Militia, 1775–76
7th Regiment of Militia, 1775–76
8th Regiment of Militia, 1775–76
8th Regiment of Militia, 1780
9th Regiment of Militia, 1776–81

10th Regiment of Militia, 1776–77
11th Regiment of Militia, 1774
12th Regiment of Militia, 1776
13th Regiment of Militia, 1776
16th Regiment of Militia, 1776
18th Regiment of Militia, 1776
20th Regiment of Militia, 1779–81
21st Regiment of Militia, 1778–81
22nd Regiment of Militia, 1776
25th Regiment of Militia, 1776–78
33rd Regiment of Militia, 1775

Belding's Regiment, 1777
Bradley's Regiment, 1776–77
Burrell's Regiment, 1776–77
Canfield's Regiment of Militia, 1781
Chapman's Regiment of Militia, 1778
Chester's Regiment of Militia, 1776–77
Cook's Regiment of Militia, 1777
Douglas' Regiment of Levies, 1776
Douglas' Regiment, 1776

Mead's Regiment of Militia, 1779
Mott's Regiment of Militia, 1776
Newberry's Regiment, 1777
Parker's Company of Teamsters, 1778
Parson's Regiment, 1776
Parson's Regiment of Militia, 1777
Porter's Regiment, 1781
Sage's Regiment, 1776–77
Silliman's Regiment, 1776

Elmore's Battalion, 1776–77
Ely's Regiment, 1777
Enos' Regiment, 1776–77
Gallup's Regiment, 1779
Gay's Regiment, 1776
Hooker's Regiment of Militia, 1777
Johnson's Regiment of Militia, 1778
Latimer's Regiment of Militia, 1777–78
Lewis' Regiment, 1776
Mason's Regiment of Militia, 1778
McClellan's Regiment, 1777–82

Talcott's Regiment, 1776
Thompson's Company
Thompson's Regiment, 1777
Tyler's Regiment, 1777
Ward's Regiment, 1777
Waterbury's Regiment, 1776–78
Whiting's Regiment, 1777
Wells' Regiment of Militia, 1779
Wells' Regiment, 1780–81
Wolcott's Regiment, 1776

2nd Connecticut Light Horse, 1777
5th Connecticut Light Horse, 1776–79
Backus' Regiment of Light Horse, 1776

Skinner's Regiment of Light Horse, 1776
Starr's Regiment of Light Horse, 1779
Seymour's Regiment of Light Dragoons

Delaware

1st Battalion, New Castle County, 1777
2nd Regiment, New Castle County, 1778–81
2nd Battalion of Militia, 1776
2nd Regiment of Militia, 1780

7th Regiment of Militia, 1782
Flying Camp Battalion, 1776
Kent County Militia
Latimer's Independent Company, 1776

Georgia

1st Brigade Georgia Militia
1st Regiment Georgia Militia

Emanuel's Regiment of Militia, 1781-1782

Georgia Hussars

Liberty Independent Troop, 1776

Maryland

34th Battalion of Militia, 1776
37th Battalion of Militia, 1777
Extraordinary Regiment, 1780
Flying Camp Regiment (Ewing's), 1776
Flying Camp Regiment (Griffith's), 1776

Washington County Militia Company, 1777
Marbury's Detachment, 1784
Lansdale's Detachment, 1783
Flying Camp Regiment (Richardson's), 1776

Gale's Independent Company of Artillery, 1779-1780
Smith's Artillery Companies, 1783

Massachusetts

Ancient and Honourable Artillery Company of Massachusetts
Independent Company of Cadets

1st Regiment of Militia, 1776
First Bristol Regiment, 1776-1780
1st Regiment of Guards, 1778
3rd Regiment of Militia, 1779
4th Regiment of Militia, 1777–80
18th Regiment of Militia, 1775
30th Regiment of Foot Massachusetts Militia, 1775–1781
25th Regiment of Foot Massachusetts Militia, 1775
32nd Regiment of Militia, 1775
Ashley's Regiment of Militia, 1776–77
Bailey's Regiment of Militia
Brewer's Regiment, 1776
Brooks' Regiment of Militia, 1778
Bucks of America, 1781
Bullards' Regiment of Militia, 1777
Burt's Company of Militia, 1776-1777
Cady's Regiment, 1776
Carpenter's Regiment of Militia (First Bristol Regiment)
Cary's Regiment, 1776
Cary's Regiment of Militia, 1780
Cogswell's Regiment of Militia, 1775–77
Cushing's Regiment of Militia, 1777
Denny's Regiment of Militia
Fellows' Regiment, 1775
French's Regiment, 1777
Frye's Regiment, 1775
Gage's Regiment of Militia (4th Essex County Militia Regiment), 1777

Gerrish's Regiment, 1778
Gill's Regiment of Militia, 1777
Holman's Regiment of Militia, 1777
Jacob's Regiment, 1778–79
Johnson's Regt. of Militia, 1775–1777
Hyde's Detachment of Militia, 1777
Keyes' Regiment, 1777
Leonard's Regiment of Militia
May's Regiment of Militia, 1777
Murray's Regiment of Militia, 1780
Perce's Battalion of Militia, 1779
Poor's Regiment of Militia, 1778
Porter's Regiment of Militia, 1776
Rand's Regiment of Levies, 1776
Reed's Regiment of Militia, 1777
Robinson's Regiment of Militia, 1777
Simonds' Regiment of Militia, 1776–77
Smith's Regiment of Foot, 1776
Sparhawk's Regiment of Militia, 1777
Stearns' Regiment of Militia, 1778
Storer's Regiment of Militia, 1777
Turner's Regiment, 1781
Wells' Regiment of Militia, 1777
Whitney's Regiment of Militia, 1777
Williams' Regiment of Militia, 1777
Wood's Regiment of Militia, 1778–79
Woodbridge's Regt. of Militia, 1777
Wright's Regiment of Militia, 1777

Plymouth Artillery Company, 1777

New Hampshire

Baker's Company of Volunteer, 1777
Baldwin's Regiment, 1776
Bartlett's Regiment of Militia, 1780
Bell's Regiment of Militia, 1781

Moore's Regiment of Militia, 1777
Morey's Regiment of Militia, 1777
Moulton's Regt of Militia, 1775–83
Nichols' Regiment of Militia, 1777–80

Bellow's Regiment of Militia, 1776–77
Chase's Regiment of Militia, 1776–77
Dame's Regiment, 1779–80
Drake's Regiment of Militia, 1777
Evans' Regiment of Militia, 1777
Fogg's Regiment, 1776–77
Gale's Regiment of Volunteers, 1778
Gilman's Regiment of Militia, 1776–77
Hale's Regiment of Militia, 1776–78
Hobart's Regiment of Militia, 1777
Kelley's Regiment of Volunteers, 1777–78
Lovewell's Regiment, 1778–81
McClary's Regiment of Militia, 1777–81
Mooney's Regiment of Militia, 1779–80

Peabody's N.H. State Regt, 1778–79
Poor's Regiment, 1775
Reed's Regiment, 1775
Reynold's Regiment of Militia, 1781
Scott's Battalion, 1783
Senter's Regiment, 1777–78
Stickney's Regiment of Militia, 1777
Tash's Regiment, 1776
Waldron's Regiment, 1776
Webster's Regiment, 1777–82
Welch's Regiment of Militia, 1777
Wingate's Regiment, 1776–78
Wyman's Regiment, 1776

Langdon's Company of Light Horse Volunteers, 1777–78

New Jersey

1st Regiment, Bergen County Militia, 1777–78
1st Regiment, Essex County, 1777
Battalion of Monmouth, 1777–82
1st Battalion of Somerset, 1777–81
2nd Regiment of Essex County, 1778
2nd Battalion of Hunterdon, 1777
2nd Battalion of Middlesex, 1777
2nd Battalion of Somerset, 1777–80

2nd Battalion of Somerset, 1777–80
3rd Battalion of Gloucester, 17771st
Borden's Regt, Burlington County, 1776
Chambers' Regt, Burlington Cty, 1776
Eastern Btln, Morris County, 1777–78
Forman's Regiment of Militia, 1776–80
Hankinson's Regt of Militia, 1777–79

Holmes' Battalion of Militia, Salem County, 1778
Hunt's Regiment, Burlington County, 1776
Martin's Regiment of Militia, 1776
Mehelm's Regiment, Burlington County, 1776
Newcomb's Regiment of Foot, 1776
Smith's Regiment, Burlington County, 1776
Shreve's Battalion, Burlington Militia

Randolph's Company, 1782
Reynolds' Regt, Burlington Cty, 1776
Philip's Regiment of Militia, 1777
Seely's Regiment of Militia, 1777–81
Summer's Battalion of Militia, 1776
Thomas' Btln of Essex Militia, 1776
Van Courtlandt's Battalion, 1776–80

Crane's Troops of Horse, 1780

New York

1st Battalion Grenadiers and Light Infantry, 1776
1st Regiment of Levies, 1780–81

Clyde's Regiment of Militia, 1779–83
Cooper's Regiment

2nd Regiment of Levies, 1776

3rd Regiment of Levies, 1780–83

Albany County militia

Cuyler's Regiment of Militia, 1781–8

Wemple's Regiment of Militia (2nd Albany County Militia Regiment), 1777–80

Schuyler's Regiment of Albany County Militia (Third Regiment of Albany County Militia), 1777

Vandenbergh's Regiment of Militia, 1778

Quackenbos' Regiment of Militia, 1779–80

Van Rensselaer's Regiment, 1779–81

Schuyler's Regiment of Militia, 1781–82

Van Alstyne's Regiment of Militia, 1777–81

Van Ness' Regiment of Militia, 1777–80

Graham's Regiment of Militia, 1777–79

Livingston's Regiment of Militia, 1777–81

Van Bergen's Regiment of Militia, 1777–80

Van Schoonhoven's Regiment of Militia, 1778–82

McCrea's Regiment of Levies, 1779

Van Veghten's Regiment of Militia, 1779–80

Yate's Regiment of Militia, 1779–80

Vrooman's Regiment of Militia, 1779–83

Van Woert's Regiment of Militia, 1779–80

Whiting's Regiment of Militia, 1777–81

Tryon County militia

Campbell's Battalion of Militia, 1776–82

Fisher's Regiment of Militia (3rd Tryon County Militia), 1775–81

Ulster County Militia

McClaughrey's Regiment of Ulster County Militia, 1776–81

Allison's Regiment of Militia, 1775–78

Benedict's Regiment of Militia, 1780–8

Brinckerhoff's Regiment of Militia, 1777

Budd's Regiment of Militia, 1776

Cantine's Regiment of Militia Levies, 1778–1779

Church's Regiment of Militia 1776

Webster's Regiment of Militia, 1780–82

Weissenfels' Regiment of Levies, 1781–82

Woodhull's Regiment, 1776

New York Provincial Company of Artillery, 1776

Crane's Regiment of Militia, 1779–81

Drake's (Joseph) Regt of Militia, 1776

Drake's (Samuel) Regt of Militia, 1776–1777

DuBois' Regiment of Levies, 1780

Vandenbergh's Regt of Militia, 1777

Field's Regiment of Militia, 1777–80

Freer's Regiment of Militia, 1777–79

Golden's Company of Militia, 1776

Hamman's Regt of Militia, 1777–82

Hardenburgh's Regt of Militia, 1776

Harper's Regiment of Militia, 1779

Hasbrouck's Regiment of Militia, 1777

Hathorn's Regiment of Militia, 1777–81

Hay's Regiment of Militia, 1778–80

Hearts of Oak (New York Militia), 1775

Hopkins' Regiment of Militia, 1779

Humphrey's Regt of Militia, 1776–77

Jansen's Regiment of Militia, 1779–82

Ludington's Regt of Militia, 1777–80

Morrison Company of Militia, 1776

Nicholson's Regiment, 1776

Nicoll's Regiment of Levies, 1776

Palmer's Regiment of Militia, 1776

Pawling's Regt of Levies and Militia, 1779–81

Pawling's Regiment of Militia, 1776–77

Snyder's Regt of Militia (First Regt of Ulster County Militia), 1776–82

Poughkeepsie Invincibles (4th Duchess County Regt, New York Militia)

Sacket's Westchester County Regt, 1776

Swartwout's Regiment of Militia, 1776

Thomas' Battalion of Militia, 1776–79

Van Brunt's Regiment of Militia, 1776

Van Cortlandt's Regt of Militia, 1777

Van Schaick's Battalion, 1776

Willett's Regiment of Levies, 1781–83

Williams' Regiment of Militia, 1778–81

Militia 1775 - 1780

militia
North Carolina
1780

Officer minutemen
Talliafero Company
Virginia 1776

Rifleman
1776

Rifle Corps
1778

Militia 1775 - 1780

Private
Green Mountain Boys
1776

militia
virginia
1780

2nd battalion
provincial force
New York 1775

Company of volunteers
Virginia
1775

North Carolina

1st Regiment of North Carolina Militia, 1780
2nd Regiment of North Carolina Militia, 1780
Bertie County Regiment, 1775–1783
Camden County Regiment, 1777–1783
Chowan County Regiment, 1775–1783
Currituck County Regiment, 1775–1783
Gates County Regiment, 1779–1783
Hertford County Regiment, 1775–1783
Martin County Regiment, 1775–1783
1st Pasquotank County Regiment, 1775–1783
2nd Pasquotank County Regiment, 1775–1777
Perquimans County Regiment, 1775–1783
Tyrrell County Regiment, 1775–1783
1st Battalion of Halifax Volunteers, 1776–1777
2nd Battalion of Halifax Volunteers, 1776–1777
Bute County Regiment, 1775–1779
Edgecombe County Regiment, 1775–1783
Franklin County Regiment, 1779–1783
Halifax County Regiment, 1775–1783
Martin County Regiment, 1775–1783
Nash County Regiment, 1777–1783
Northampton County Regiment, 1775–1783
Warren County Regiment, 1779–1783
Caswell County Regiment, 1777–1783
Chatham County Regiment, 1775–1783
Granville County Regiment, 1775–1783
Northern Orange County Regiment, 1776–1777
Orange County Regiment, 1775–1783
Randolph County Regiment, 1779–1783
Wake County Regiment, 1775–1783
Beaufort County Regiment, 1775–1783
Bladen County Regiment, 1775–1783
Brunswick County Regiment, 1775–1783
Cumberland County Regiment, 1775–1783
Duplin County Regiment, 1775–1783

Carteret County Regiment, 1775–1783
Craven County Regiment, 1775–1783
Dobbs County Regiment, 1775–1783
Hyde County Regiment, 1775–1783
Johnston County Regiment, 1775–1783
Jones County Regiment, 1779–1783
Pitt County Regiment, 1775–1783
Wayne County Regiment, 1779–1783
Davidson County Regiment, 1783
Green County Regiment, 1783
Anson County Regiment, 1775–1783
Burke County Regiment, 1777–1782
Guilford County Regiment, 1775–1783
Lincoln County Regiment, 1779–1783
1st Mecklenburg Cty Regt, 1775–1783
2nd Mecklenburg Cty Regt, 1779–1780
Montgomery County Regt, 1779–1783
Richmond County Regt, 1779–1783
Rowan County Regiment, 1775–1783
2nd Rowan County Regt, 1775–1777
2nd Rowan County Regt, 1782–1783
Rutherford County Regt, 1779–1783
Sullivan County Regiment, 1779–1783
Surry County Regiment, 1775–1783
Tryon County Regiment, 1775–1779
Washington District Regt, 1776–1777
Washington District Regt, 1777–1783
Wilkes County Regiment, 1777–1783
1st Battalion of Wilmington Militia,
    1776-1776
2nd Battalion of Wilmington Militia,
    1776-1776
Onslow County Regiment, 1775–1783
New Hanover County Regt, 1775–1783

Polk's Regiment of Light Dragoons, 1779–1780
Mounted Volunteers Regiment, 1780

Independent corps of light horse, 1780

Pennsylvania

Associated Regiment of Foot of Philadelphia
1st Battalion Flying Camp, 1776
1st Battalion of Chester County Militia, 1776–77
1st Battalion of Cumberland County Militia, 1776–77
1st Regiment Flying Camp of Lancaster County, 1776
1st Battalion of Philadelphia County Militia, 1776
1st Battalion of Riflemen, Philadelphia Cty Militia, 1776
1st Battalion of Westmoreland County Militia, 1777
2nd Regiment Flying Camp, 1776
2nd Battalion of Cumberland County Militia, 1776–1777
2nd Battalion of Northampton County Militia, 1778
2nd Battalion of Riflemen, Lancaster County, 1776–77
2nd Battalion of Westmoreland County Militia, 1777
3rd Battalion of Chester County Militia, 1776–77
3rd Battalion of Cumberland County Militia, 1776
3rd Battalion of Lancaster County Militia, 1776
3rd Battalion of the Northhampton County Militia,
    1777–84
3rd Battalion of Northumberland County Militia, 1779
3rd Battalion of Washington County Militia, 1779–83
4th Battalion of Chester County Militia, 1776
4th Battalion of Philadelphia County Militia, 1776
5th Battalion of Chester County Militia, 1776
5th Battalion of Philadelphia County Militia, 1776
5th Battalion of York County Militia, 1777
Andrews' Battalion of York County Militia, 1777–78
Schott's Independent Corps, 1778
Swope's Regiment Flying Camp, 1776–80

Atlee's Musket Battalion, 1777
Baxter's Battalion Flying Camp, 1776
Barr's Detachment of Westmoreland
    County Militia, 1778
Clugage's Battalion, 1778
Burd's Battalion, 1776
Clotz's Battalion Flying Camp,
    Lancaster County, 1776
Duncan's Company of Volunteers
    (Pittsburgh), 1778
Enslow's Company of Bedford County
    Militia, 1782–83
Ferreis' Battalion of Militia (Lancaster
    County), 1776
Haller's Battalion Flying Camp, 1776
Hart's Btlnn of Bucks Cty Militia, 1776
Matlack's Rifle Battalion, 1777
Miles' Rifle Regiment, 1776
Lochny's Battalion
Militia of York County
Moorhead's Independent Company,
    1777–79
Quaker Blues
Rankin's Regiment of York County
    Militia, 1777
Reed's Volunteers, 1780–81
Watt's Regiment Flying Camp, 1776

1st Troop Philadelphia City Cavalry, 1774

Philadelphia Light Horse Troop, 1780

Artillery Battalion, Pennsylvania Militia

Rhode Island

1st Regiment Providence County Militia, 1781
2nd Regiment Providence County Militia, 1781
15th Regiment of Rhode Island Militia, 1775
Babcock's Regiment of Militia, 1776–77
Bowen's Regiment of Militia, 1778

Miller's Regiment of Militia, 1778
North Providence Rangers, 1775
Noyes' Regiment of Militia, 1777–78
Olney's Regiment of Militia, 1781
Pawtuxet Rangers, 1774

Cook's Regiment of Militia, 1777
Crary's Regiment, 1777–79
Kentish Guards, 1774
Kimball's Regiment of Militia, 1781
Lippitt's Regiment, 1776
Mathewson's Regiment, 1778

Peck's Regiment, 1780–81
Porter's Regiment of Militia, 1781
Richmond's Regiment, 1775–1777
Tillinghast's Regiment, 1781
Topham's Regiment, 1778–80
Waterman's Regiment, 1776–88

Artillery Company of Westerly, Charlestown
   and Hopkinton
Bristol Train of Artillery, 1776

Elliott's Regiment of Artillery, 1776–78
Newport Artillery Company
United Train of Artillery, 1775

South Carolina

Beaufort District Regiment, 1778
Berkeley County Regiment, 1775
Camden District Regiment, 1775
Casey's Regiment, 1782
Catawba Indian Company of Rovers, 1775–1776
Cheraws District Regiment, 1775
Charles Town District Regiment, 1775
Colleton County Regiment, 1775
Lower District Regiment (aka Dutch Fork Regt), 1776
German Fusiliers of Charleston, 1775

Craven County Regiment, 1775
Lower Craven County Regiment, 1775
Upper Craven County Regiment, 1775
Fairfield Regiment, 1775
Forks of Saluda District Regiment, 1775
Georgetown District Regiment, 1775
Graville County Regiment, 1775–1780
Lower Granville County Regt, 1775
Upper Graville County Regiment, 1775

Horse Guards
Charles Town Artillery Company, 1775

Vermont (autonomous territory)

6th Regiment of militia, 1780–1781
7th Regiment of militia, 1782
Abbott's Regiment of militia, 1781
Clark's Company of militia, 1778–1780
Durkee's Company of militia, 1780–1781
Herrick's Regiment, 1775–83
Hoar's Company of militia, 1780

Marsh's Regiment, 1777
Mattison's Company of militia, 1782
Mead's Regiment of militia, 1777
Robbinson's Regt of militia, 1776–1777
Weld's Company of militia, 1780
White's Company of militia, 1781

Virginia

Virginia Legion
Culpeper Minutemen, 1775–1776
Volunteers, 1783–1784

Gaskin's Virginia Battalion, 1781
Illinois Regiment of Virginia
Monongalia County Militia, 1777

Dabney's State Legion, 1782-1783
Ford's Company of militia, 1777
Frederick County Militia, 1777
Fluvanna County Militia, 1781

Pendleton's Regiment of Militia, 1777
Taylor's Regt of Militia (Albemarle Cty), 1779
Virginia State Regiment, 1775–83
Western Battalion, 1781–82

Captain Johnson's Company of Mounted Militia (Augusta County), 1780

The many of the militia units and state troops listed above did not play a significant role during the American Revolution, since they only garrisoned their home territories or supported the Continental Army for very short periods of time. There were, however, some notable exceptions to this general rule. The "minutemen" of 1775, for example, were all militiamen with little or no proper training to speak of but their contribution was essential during the early battles of the war. Basically a "minuteman" was a militiaman who could be called out to serve at a minute's notice and who was ready to rush where needed even without receiving official orders. The minutemen of the Massachusetts Militia were the first American soldiers who fought against the British Army and showed their deadly capabilities as marksmen at the battles of Concord and Lexington. In 1774 the Massachusetts Militia comprised a total of seven infantry regiments, who had been progressively purged of all the officers who were loyal to the Crown; these all comprised some "alarm units" of minutemen, which were formed from each militia company. One-third of the men in each single company, in fact, were minutemen who could be mobilized very rapidly to face an imminent threat. Units of minutemen were formed also outside Massachusetts, most notably in Virginia: in the latter colony, for example, the famous "Culpeper Minute Battalion" was organized in July 1775. This consisted of six companies with 50 militiamen each and was disbanded in January 1776 after having participated to several engagements.

It is interesting to note that several militia units bore the denomination of "flying camp"; the latter expression was used by the same George Washington to indicate a mobile and strategic reserve of local troops that could defend a specific territory from enemy attacks. In practice, the "flying camps" were an evolution of the early minutemen units. In June 1776, after the British evacuation of Boston, the Second Continental Congress decided to organize a large flying camp with 10,000 militiamen for protection of the middle colonies. Washington, in fact, feared that the British could organize a massive landing in that theatre of operations but could not garrison the latter with his own Continental Army. This first flying camp served until December 1776 and comprised militiamen from three different

American militiamen from different units; the cavalryman on the right is from the Philadelphia City Troop of Light Horse.

colonies: 6,000 from Pennsylvania, 3,400 from Maryland and 600 from Delaware. The Maryland and Virginia Rifle Regiment of the Continental Army was partly recruited from former members of this early flying camp. The German Battalion of the Continentals was initially created as part of this little-known military force. With the progression of the hostilities several new and smaller "flying camp" units were raised by the single states, as part of their militias.

Most of the militia units and state troops consisted of infantry, but some smaller corps of cavalry and artillery did also exist. Cavalry units were very expensive to equip and support, while artillery ones needed enough guns and some expert officers. Despite this, some of the southern states were able to field excellent light cavalry corps and some of the northern ones were able to organize effective artillery companies. Among the best cavalry corps, we should mention the Philadelphia City Troop of Light Horse of the Pennsylvania Militia (which even served as Washington's mounted bodyguard), the Baltimore Light Dragoons of the Maryland Militia, the Light Horse Regiment of the South Carolina Militia and the State Regiment of Light Dragoons of South Carolina. Members of these units were mostly gentlemen, who were responsible for providing their own uniforms and equipment as well as for taking care of their personal horses. Among the best artillery corps, we should mention the Massachusetts Artillery Regiment (with ten batteries and one artificer company, later transformed into the Continental Artillery Regiment), the Rhode Island Train of Artillery (one company, later absorbed into the Continental Artillery Regiment), the Virginia Artillery Regiment and the South Carolina Artillery Regiment (with three companies/batteries, later augmented to six). Among the various states, Virginia was with no doubts the one having the best state troops; these included three small corps that were specifically created for service against the natives in the frontier areas: the Illinois Troop of Light Dragoons (a unit of mounted rangers), the Frontier Independent Company (a unit of foot rangers) and Captain de la Porte's Company (an infantry corps made up of French volunteers). In January 1782 Virginia consolidated the remnants of her state troops into a large unit known as "Virginia State Legion", which was commanded by Charles Dabney. This garrisoned the cities of Richmond, Hampton and Yorktown until being disbanded in April 1783. Most of the states also had their own "state navies" for defence of their coastline and these, albeit small, could be used to contrast the raids of the Royal Navy; in addition, there were also some small corps of Marines that were part of these "state navies" in Maryland, Pennsylvania and Virginia.

When the hostilities with Great Britain began, "The Associators" of Pennsylvania reorganized their military forces and expanded them very rapidly. By the end of the American Revolution, these comprised the following corps: four-line infantry battalions, one rifle battalion, one artillery battalion and one battalion of "City Guards" (tasked with keeping order in the city of Philadelphia). Each of the line infantry battalions included an elite light company and all the units organized by "The Associators" were re-trained by Baron von Steuben like the regulars of the Continental Army (after being assembled into a "Philadelphia Brigade" commanded by General Cadwalader during 1777). To conclude this overview of the most notable militia units and state troops of the American Revolution, we should give some details about another two-notable corps: the "Bucks of America" of the Massachusetts Militia and the "Hearts of Oak" (also known as "The Corsicans") of the New York Militia. The first was an infantry company entirely made up of African-American volunteers, being one of the few "segregated" units created during the American Revolution. Since 1775 black soldiers, both slaves and freemen, could be found in several militia units of the New England colonies; in the Continental Army, instead, the inclusion of black soldiers always remained controversial due to the strong opposition to this measure that was expressed by the southern colonies. After the British offered freedom to all the slaves who would escape from their American masters to join their cause, George Washington permitted the enlistment of free blacks in the Continental Army. White owners could enrol their slaves, as substitutes, for their own service. The Bucks of America were mostly employed as a police force and patrolled the city of Boston, where they had been raised. The Hearts of Oak were a volunteer company raised in New York, mostly from students of the King's College (now Columbia University). Their nickname, "The Corsicans", derived from the fact that these young volunteers had a great sympathy for the patriots of the Corsican Republic (1755-1769). The latter, under guidance of Pasquale Paoli, had fought with great courage against the French in order to preserve the independence of Corsica but had been finally defeated after a desperate struggle. The members of the Hearts of Oak trained every day before classes and had as their peculiar motto the famous expression "Liberty or Death". In general terms, we could say that without the support of the militias and of the state troops the Continental Army would have never been able to defeat the British; it should be remembered, however, that actual fighting was just a minor component of this support due to the limited combat capabilities of the militias and state troops.

Ranks and Insignia

The American military forces adopted many of the distinctions that the British military forces used to show a soldier's rank. In his effort to create a professional military force, Gen. Washington tried to emulate these insignias of rank and introduced them into the Continental Army. Corporals and Sergeants wore a fringed woolen epaulette (often in the facing colour of their coat) on the right shoulder. Officers were distinguished by epaulettes of lace and wire; lower-rank officers had silver epaulettes; senior-rank officers had golden epaulettes. The system of ranks for officers was:

Lieutenants had an epaulette on the left shoulder.
Captains had an epaulette on the right shoulder.
Majors had two epaulettes.
Lieutenant Colonels and Colonels had two epaulettes with bolder fringe.
Brigadier Generals had two epaulettes with a star on each.
Major Generals had two epaulettes with two stars on each.

In addition, both NCOs and officers would often wear a sash either around the waist or across the shoulder. NCOs might also be allowed to carry a small sword and/or a spontoon or pike to direct and control troops on the field.

Epaulettes of an officer. An epaulette of a NCO would have been worn singularly and would have been made of worsted wool.

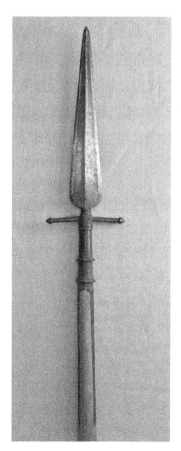

(Left) a pike used by an officer or NCO from the Revolutionary War.

(Top) George Washington's epaulettes

(Right) A spontoon based on the British pattern used by American forces

Flags and Standards

Because the American military units were organized similarly to their British equivalents, regiments were supposed to have two flags: a "national" flag and a "state" or "unit" flag. There was no standard "national" flag throughout the period of the American Revolution. The Grand Union flag, which still incorporated bits of the Union Jack, was used by Washington since 1775. The First Resolution Flag authorized by Congress was first introduced in 1777 and featured the "stars and stripes". Variations of the Resolution Flag were used in different theaters by different commanders. State or regimental flags took various forms. Early in the war, many of these incorporated the Union Jack, but as the war went on some of them took the form of the state flags as they are seen today.

The Grand Union Flag 1775

The First Resolution Flag 1777

The Bennington Flag

George Washington's Life Guard

The Gilford Courthouse Fag flown by North Carolina militia

Flag of the 1st New Jersey Regiment

Gabriele Esposito

Color Plates

Figure A

Figure B

B2

B1

B3

C3

C2

C1

Figure D

D1

D2

D3

Figure E

F2

F3

F1

Figure G

H1

H3

H2

Commentaries to the uniform plates

Militias and state troops

The pre-war militias of the Thirteen Colonies sometimes had no uniforms and thus their members wore their civilian clothing when serving. This was generally quite simple and differed a lot according to the geographical provenance of a militiaman. The militiamen coming from large urban settlements looked quite similar to the Boston militiaman reproduced in **figure A1**. The latter is wearing a simple black tricorn and a brown coat, together with white waistcoat and trousers. White stockings and a pair of short black leather boots complete his outfit. Personal equipment was usually reduced to a minimum, comprising just a leather ammunition pouch and a white canvas haversack. Only some men also had a metal canteen. All American militiamen, however, were armed with excellent muskets. These could be smoothbores or "Kentucky" rifles, the latter being very popular among the militiamen coming from frontier communities. Rifles had a longer barrel and were much more accurate than the smoothbore muskets; they were, however, quite difficult to maintain in a good state and needed more time to reload than the smoothbores. The militiamen coming from the countryside and from the frontier settlements were dressed in a different way and their distinctive piece of cloth was the fringed "hunting shirt". The latter was worn by mountain men and trappers, being extremely comfortable and easy to produce. **Figure A2** represents a "minuteman" from the Minute Battalion of Culpeper County. This Virginian is wearing a hunting shirt that has been dyed in dark green and dark blue leggings; the latter were extremely popular for use on campaign and were "copied" from those worn by the natives. The headgear is a round hat with white plume. Personal equipment includes a horn with the black powder, a hunting knife and a hatchet. The officers of the Minute Battalion of Culpeper County wore a different and more "conventional" uniform, consisting of the following elements: black tricorn edged in white, dark green coat with horizontal pockets on the sides and dark blue leggings. Not all militia units, however, were dressed with their civilian clothing; several corps, especially those performing specific functions or those made up of wealthy gentlemen, wore elegant uniforms that were clearly influenced by the contemporary British military fashion. This was the case, for example, of the Baltimore Independent Cadets who were dressed like **figure E1**. Before the outbreak of the American Revolution, red uniforms were very popular in the Thirteen Colonies and some of them continued to be worn by the militia corps also during the conflict. The NCO represented in our plate was easily distinguishable from his men thanks to three elements: the red sash worn around the waist, the silver "epaulette" worn on the left shoulder and the use of a "spontoon" as main weapon. The ranks of officers and NCOs were shown by the golden or silver "epaulettes" and "contre-epaulettes" applied on the shoulders; the latter were "epaulettes" without fringes. Sometimes the edging of the tricorn could be golden or silver in order to match with the "epaulettes" and "contre-epaulettes". Officers used a red sash like the NCOs, but instead of wearing it around the waist they wore it over the right shoulder. Most of the NCOs were armed with ordinary muskets, since "spontoons" like the one represented in our plate were used only by the sergeants who were tasked with protecting the colours of their unit. The main weapon of the officers was the sword, which was carried also by some NCOs. All the rank distinctions described above were introduced, without modifications, also in the new Continental Army. Sometimes the uniforms of the militia units could comprise just a few "common" pieces of cloth, like in the case of **figure A3** that reproduces a militiaman from Virginia: he is wearing a black tricorn and a dark blue coat with green facings together with his civilian clothing. On campaign, especially during winter, the frontal lapels of the coat could be buttoned-up and thus look as a double-breasted coat. When not used, greatcoats could be worn around the torso for additional protection against enemy bayonets, like in our figure. A good number of militia units had peculiar uniforms that were quite different from those of the Continental Army; this was the case, most notably, of the cavalry and artillery corps but also of some light infantry ones.

Figure F3 represents a light infantryman from the Dover Light Infantry Company, which was part of the 1st Battalion Kent County of the Delaware Militia. Due to its great discipline and smart uniform, this corps was honoured with the privilege of acting as Washington's "additional" personal bodyguard after the American victories of Trenton and Princeton in New Jersey. The Dover Light Infantry wore a short dark green coat with red lapels and round cuffs; the black "jockey cap" and the "belly box" cartridge pouch were quite peculiar for a light infantry corps, since they were usually worn by light cavalry units and not by foot ones. Among the various militia units, those organized by "The Associators" of Philadelphia were with no doubts among the best dressed. The light companies of the four infantry battalions were uniformed like **figure F1**, with black "jockey cap" and a short dark green coat with lapels/round cuffs in the distinctive colour of each unit. Waistcoat and breeches were white. Soldiers of the line companies were dressed in the same way, but their coats were dark brown and not green. The distinctive colours of the four battalions were buff for the 1st, red for the 2nd, white for the 3rd and yellow for the 4th. The battalion of riflemen had the same black "jockey cap" of the other units but wore fringed hunting shirt and leggings made of brown leather. The Philadelphia City Troop of Light Horse was dressed in brown like the infantry battalions of "The Associators". Its uniform consisted of the following elements: black "jockey cap" with white crest and light blue sash wrapped around the bottom part, having black leather peak and frontal plate (the latter edged in white); dark brown coat with white lapels and round cuffs, white waistcoat, buff breeches and black leather boots. The cavalry corps of the militias and state troops were all uniformed more or less in the same way, with "Tarleton" crested helmets and coloured short coats. This kind of light cavalry dress is represented in **figure F2**, which reproduces the uniform of the Virginia State Legion's light dragoons. In this case the helmet is entirely black and the lapels of the coat are not in contrasting colour. The infantry of the Virginia State Legion had the same helmet of the light dragoons, but wore a single-breasted green jacket and dark blue leggings. The Baltimore Light Dragoons had a black "jockey cap" with a black leather frontal plate edged in white (having the letters "L" and "H" embroidered in white on the front) and a dark blue band wrapped around the bottom part. Dark grey single-breasted coat with no frontal lapels, having dark blue folded collar and round cuffs. White waistcoat, buff breeches and black leather boots. The Light Horse Regiment of the South Carolina Militia was dressed as follows: black "jockey cap" with a black leather frontal plate and a light blue band wrapped around the bottom part. Dark blue single-breasted coat with no frontal lapels, having light blue folded collar and round cuffs. White waistcoat and breeches, black leather boots. The State Regiment of Light Dragoons from South Carolina was dressed as follows: black "jockey cap" with a black leather frontal plate and a red band wrapped around the bottom part. Dark brown coat with red frontal lapels and pointed cuffs, light brown waistcoat and breeches, black leather boots. The Rhode Island Train of Artillery wore a black leather "light infantry" cap with frontal plate embroidered in gold, dark brown coat with red frontal lapels and round cuffs, white waistcoat and breeches. The Virginia Artillery Regiment had black tricorn with black cockade, dark blue coat with black frontal lapels and round cuffs, dark blue waistcoat and breeches. The South Carolina Artillery Regiment wore black "jockey cap" with a black leather frontal plate and a red band wrapped around the bottom part. Dark blue coat with red frontal lapels and round cuffs, dark blue waistcoat and grey overalls. The frontier units of the Virginia Militia were dressed in a quite peculiar way. The Illinois Troop of Light Dragoons initially wore a black round hat and a brown leather hunting shirt, together with white leggings; later they received a more "regular" uniform, which comprised the following elements: black "jockey cap" with a black leather frontal plated edged in white and a red band wrapped around the bottom part, dark blue single-breasted coat without frontal lapels and with white piping to folded collar and round cuffs, dark blue waistcoat piped in white, light blue leggings. Members of this corps, like all frontiersmen, used comfortable moccasins instead of the standard shoes or boots. The Frontier Independent Company was uniformed with grey soft cap, dark brown coat with yellow frontal lapels and round cuffs, light brown waistcoat and leggings. Captain de la Porte's Company had a French-style uniform: black tricorn edged in white, dark blue coat with red frontal lapels and dark blue round cuffs, buff waistcoat and breeches.

Continental line infantry

As explained in the previous chapters, the Continental Army was formed by assembling together the many militiamen who were already fighting against the British around Boston and New York. As a result, it initially consisted of regiments that had no proper uniforms to speak of: most of the early Continentals were dressed in their civilian clothes and hunting shirts were extremely popular. Very soon, however, the newly established "regiments of the line" started to have their own distinctive uniforms. These consisted of some basic elements, which were common to all units: a black tricorn and a coat in regimental colour having frontal lapels and round cuffs in a contrasting colour. Since each regiment had the coat in a distinctive colour, the early Continental Army presented a very motley appearance. Dark blue soon became the most popular colour for coats but also dark brown was extremely common to find during this early phase (due to its low costs of production). Red, instead, was the most common colour for frontal lapels and round cuffs. Some units, like the Delaware Regiment of the Line represented in **figure E2**, had smart uniforms since their foundation. This unit, in particular, wore a peculiar light infantry cap instead of the usual tricorn. The rest of the dress, in dark blue with red facings, was not different from that of many other regiments. Waistcoat and breeches were white for most of the units and were worn together with white gaiters and black leather shoes/short boots. Belt equipment was white for all corps. By the end of 1776 most of the Continental infantry was dressed like **figure B1**: black tricorn with yellow or white edging, dark blue coat with red frontal lapels and round cuffs, white waistcoat, white or buff trousers and black shoes. There were, however, several "exceptions" to this rule since no official dress regulations did exist. The Green Mountain Rangers of Vermont, for example, were dressed as follows: black tricorn with black cockade, dark green coat with red folded collar and round cuffs, buff waistcoat and breeches. The 1st Continental Regiment, being a rifle unit, had the following dress: black light infantry cap with the word "CONGRESS" embroidered in white on the front and adorned with white plumes, white fringeless hunting shirt, white leggings, and black shoes. The Maryland and Virginia Rifle Regiment was uniformed quite similarly to the 1st Continental Regiment: black round hat, white fringed hunting shirt, white leggings, and black shoes. This informal dress was used also by the Provisional Rifle Corps. Like most of the early units of the Continental infantry, the two Canadian regiments created during the failed US invasion of Quebec were dressed in dark brown. This uniform is reproduced in **figure E3**; it consisted of black tricorn, dark brown coat with frontal lapels and round cuffs in regimental colour, white waistcoat, and breeches. The black light infantry cap shown in our plate was used only by the light companies. Regimental colour was white for the 1st Canadian Regiment and red for the 2nd Canadian Regiment. The German Battalion was dressed similarly to the Canadian Regiments, in dark brown, but had green as regimental colour. Drummers of all the Continental infantry regiments had uniforms with inverted colours, to be easy to recognize on the battlefield. Since red was the most popular "contrasting" colour for infantry coats, most of the drummers were uniformed in red. The latter was used as facing colour and not as main colour by most of the units to avoid confusion, since all the British infantry regiments wore red coats. The "additional" infantry regiments raised by George Washington during 1777 were dressed like the standard ones, but some of them could have a few peculiar features: several of these units, for example, wore a black round hat as headgear instead of the tricorn; in addition, most of the "additional" regiments were dressed in dark brown coats and not with the more common dark blue ones. Sometimes, as for other Continental regiments, the tricorn could be replaced by a black light infantry cap decorated with plumes. Since the beginning, Washington tried to introduce some degree of uniformity inside his Continental Army, but he was able to obtain some significant results in this sense only with the few units that were under his direct command. During 1774, in Fairfax County (Virginia), the future Commander-in-Chief of the Continental Army had organized a company of volunteer militiamen dressed in dark blue coats having buff facings. After becoming supreme commander of US military forces, Washington continued to wear the uniform of his company and ordered to the officers of his General Staff to adopt it as their standard dress. As a result, superior officers of the Continental Army were uniformed as follows: black tricorn with black-and-white cockade and white plume, dark blue coat with buff frontal lapels and round cuffs, golden "epaulettes" on the shoulders, buff waistcoat and breeches, black leather boots.

The Commander-in-Chief's Guard, organized in March 1776, was dressed in this "blue and buff" uniform as can be seen from **figure B2** of the colour plates. The first headgear employed by this small elite corps was a black tricorn edged in white and having a white-and-black cockade; with the progression of time, however, the latter was replaced by the distinctive "Tarleton" helmet reproduced in our plate (with dark blue band wrapped around the bottom part and blue-and-white plume). The red "contre-epaulette" on the right shoulder was a "mark of distinction" of this elite corps, like the red waistcoat. The Provost Corps, created during 1778, was uniformed quite similarly to the Commander-in-Chief's Guard: black leather helmet with a band of brown fur wrapped around the bottom part and black horsehair tail, dark blue coat with yellow frontal lapels and round cuffs, buff waistcoat and trousers, black leather boots. Members of the Invalid Corps, instead, wore the uniforms of the regiments to which they had belonged while on active service. As time progressed, the bulk of the Continental infantry started to be dressed in dark blue coats but many regimental variations continued to exist; light infantry caps became increasingly popular and several units started to add some coloured lace on the buttonholes of their coats' frontal lapels and round cuffs. Among the various regiments of the Continental Infantry, the Rhode Island Regiment of the Line wore one of the most elegant uniforms; this comprised the following elements: black light infantry cap piped in white and with a white anchor embroidered on the front, dark blue coat with white frontal lapels and pointed cuffs, white waistcoat and trousers, black shoes. When Washington decided to introduce the first official dress regulations for his Continental Army, the uniform of the Rhode Island Regiment of the Line was taken as an example.

The Commander-in-Chief wanted to introduce a smart "universal" uniform, comfortable to wear and simple to produce, that could have been worn by all the infantry regiments of the Continental Army. To achieve this objective and to eliminate in a definitive way the many regimental distinctions that still existed, in October 1779 the first dress regulations in the history of the US military forces were promulgated. These were heavily influenced by the contemporary military fashions of the French Army, which dress was the most elegant in the world. France was the main ally of the USA in that moment and thus would have provided enough cloth/accoutrements to produce the new uniforms quite rapidly. The new M1779 dress of the Continental infantry consisted of the following elements: black tricorn with white edging and black-and-white cockade, dark blue coat with frontal lapels and round cuffs in distinctive colour, white waistcoat and trousers, black shoes. Distinctive colours were four in total and were assigned to the various regiments according to their area: white for the units of Massachusetts, New Hampshire, Connecticut, and Rhode Island; buff for the units of New York and New Jersey; red for the units of Virginia, Pennsylvania, Maryland, and Delaware; dark blue (with buttonholes trimmed with white tape or worsted lace) for the units of North Carolina, South Carolina, and Georgia. Since May 1778, each infantry regiment was ordered to comprise a light infantry company; the latter was usually dressed like the rest of its "mother" unit but replaced the standard tricorn with a black light infantry cap and wore distinctive "wings" made of cloth on the shoulders. The cap could be of several different shapes and could be decorated in many alternative ways. With the introduction of the M1779 uniforms the light infantry companies continued to wear their distinctive caps and "wings" but adopted the same dress of the line companies. **Figure B3** of the colour plates represents a soldier from a light infantry company wearing the distinctive light infantry cap of his regiment (in this case the 4th Massachusetts Regiment of the Line) and white "wings" on the shoulders. All the light infantry companies of the Continental Army that were assembled into the "Light Infantry Division" of Lafayette were given a black-and-red distinctive plume, which was worn by single soldiers on their caps as shown in figure B3. With the new dress regulations of 1779, all musicians continued to have uniforms with reversed colours; most of them, in addition, replaced the tricorn with the cap worn by the light infantry company of their regiment. The Continental infantry adopted the new uniforms very slowly and for long time the old dress remained in use; by the end of the hostilities, however, most of the regiments had a regular and neat appearance.

Cavalry, technical corps, partisan units and Marines

The 1st Regiment of Continental Light Dragoons was dressed in dark brown with green facings, as shown in **figure C1** of the colour plates; the 2nd Regiment of Continental Light Dragoons, instead, wore the following uniform: brass helmet having a crest covered by a white plume and a light blue band wrapped around the bottom part, dark blue coat with buff frontal lapels and pointed cuffs, buff waistcoat and dark brown breeches. The 3rd Regiment of Continental Light Dragoons was dressed in white with light blue facings, as shown in **figure C2**, while the 4th Regiment was uniformed in red with dark blue facings, as represented in **figure C3**. The first three units of light dragoons all had "provisional" uniforms with different colours before adopting the definitive ones described above. Trumpeters of all four units wore uniforms with inverted colours. Since the beginning of the American Revolution, the uniforms of the Continental artillery were very similar to those of the line infantry. The 1st Continental Artillery Regiment, raised in Massachusetts, was dressed in dark blue with buff facings; the 2nd Continental Artillery Regiment, instead, was uniformed in dark blue with red facings. When the Continental Artillery was reorganized and expanded on four regiments, it received the new "unified" uniform that is represented in **figure D1**: black tricorn with black-and-white cockade, dark blue coat with red frontal lapels and round cuffs, white waistcoat and trousers, black shoes. The few officers of the Engineer Corps were dressed in "blue and buffs" exactly like those of Washington's General Staff; also, the Sappers and Miners Corps wore dark blue coats with buff facings, as shown by **figure D3**. The Artillery Artificer Regiment had the same uniform of the artillery regiments, comprising dark blue coat with red facings; in **figure D2** we have represented the dress worn by the commanding officer of the unit, having additional golden embroidering on the coat and waistcoat. The Partisan Corps of the Continental Army had peculiar uniforms that reflected the "national" provenance of their members. Armand's Legion wore a dark blue coat with buff frontal lapels and round cuffs, together with buff trousers. This dress, shown in **figure G1**, could be worn with the frontal lapels of the coat buttoned up. The headgear for cavalrymen was a "Tarleton" helmet with black crest, while the headgear for infantrymen was a black light infantry cap. The infantry and light dragoons of Pulaski's Legion wore the elegant uniform shown in **figure G2** of the colour plates; the lancers, instead, had the same black helmet but wore a dark blue single-breasted jacket with yellow piping to the pointed cuffs and white frontal frogging. The jacket was worn over a buff waistcoat with yellow piping; buff breeches and black leather boots completed the uniform. Lee's Legion was initially dressed with black "Tarleton" helmet, buff coat with dark green frontal lapels and round cuffs, buff breeches and black leather boots. When the unit was expanded and started to comprise also some infantrymen, the new dress reproduced in **figure G3** was introduced. Obviously, cavalrymen had black leather boots and infantrymen simple black shoes. The Continental Marines had a very peculiar uniform, comprising black round hat and dark green coat with white facings; this is shown in **figure H3** of the colour plates. In 1779 the facing colour was changed from white to red. The Maryland State Marines wore black tricorn, light blue hunting shirt and buff breeches; the Pennsylvania State Marines were dressed in black tricorn edged in white, dark brown coat with green facings, white waistcoat, and buff breeches; the Virginia State Marines had black tricorn, buff hunting shirt and brown breeches. The uniforms of the Continental Navy were similar to those of the contemporary Royal Navy, as shown by **figure H1**; their facing colour, however, was to be red according to official regulations (and not white, as in the non-regulation dress reproduced in our plate). Continental sailors had no uniform to speak of, as clear from the dress of the "midshipman" reproduced in **figure H2**. Black round hats and white trousers, however, were worn by most of the sailors.

Appendix: Continental Army's Uniforms and Equipment

Continental infantrymen firing their smoothbore muskets in line, according to contemporary European tactics. *Photo by the 1ˢᵗ Virginia Regiment of the Continental Line.*

Continental infantrymen firing in close formation, at the order of a NCO. Some of them are wearing hunting shirts. *Photo by Dr. Eric Nason, 2ⁿᵈ South Carolina Regiment.*

Soldiers of the 1st Virginia Regiment of the Continental Line. According to the 1779 dress regulations, regiments from Virginia were to have red facings. *Photo by the 1st Virginia Regiment of the Continental Line.*

Soldiers of the 1st Virginia Regiment of the Continental Line. According to the 1779 dress regulations, regiments from Virginia were to have red facings. *Photo by the 1st Virginia Regiment of the Continental Line.*

Left: Lieutenant of the 2nd South Carolina Regiment of the Continental Line, wearing pre-1779 uniform. *Photo by Dr. Eric Nason, 2nd South Carolina Regiment.*

Right: NCO of the 2nd South Carolina Regiment of the Continental Line. This unit had as headgear a distinctive light infantry cap, which was worn instead of the usual tricorn. *Photo by Dr. Eric Nason, 2nd South Carolina Regiment*

Soldier of the 2nd North Carolina Regiment of the Continental Line. Each Continental infantryman wore two crossbelts made of white leather: one for the black ammunition pouch and one for the bayonet scabbard. *Photo by Dr. Eric Nason, 2nd South Carolina Regiment.*

Soldier of the Delaware Regiment of the Continental Line. Initially this unit had a light infantry cap as headgear, like the 2nd South Carolina Regiment; at a certain point, however, this was replaced by the standard tricorn shown here. *Photo by Dr. Eric Nason, 2nd South Carolina Regiment.*

Drummer of the 2nd South Carolina Regiment of the Continental Line. All musicians wore uniforms with reversed colours, in this case red with dark blue facings. *Photo by Dr. Eric Nason, 2nd South Carolina Regiment.*

Rifleman serving with the 2nd South Carolina Regiment of the Continental Line, with white hunting shirt. *Photo by Dr. Eric Nason, 2nd South Carolina Regiment.*

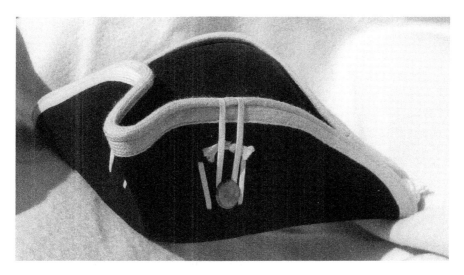

The tricorn of a line infantryman, with white edging and black-and-white cockade. *Photo by Dr. Eric Nason, 2nd South Carolina Regiment.*

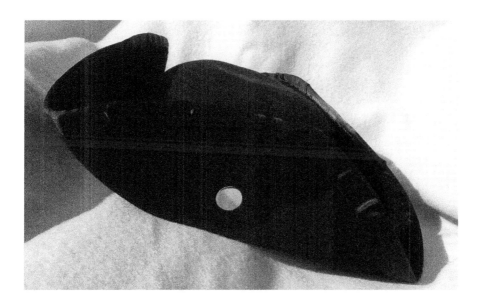

A simple black tricorn, without edging, of the model worn by most militiamen and Continentals during the early years of the American Revolution. *Photo by Dr. Eric Nason, 2nd South Carolina Regiment.*

The light infantry cap worn by the 2nd South Carolina Regiment of the Continental Line. Made of leather, it had a crescent-shaped metal badge on the front bearing the word "LIBERTY". *Photo by Dr. Eric Nason, 2nd South Carolina Regiment.*

Cap of the Portsmouth Light Infantry

The coat used by a lieutenant of the 2nd South Carolina Regiment of the Continental Line. Rank is shown by the silver "epaulette" applied on the right shoulder. *Photo by Dr. Eric Nason, 2nd South Carolina Regiment.*

The coat used by a drummer of the 2nd South Carolina Regiment of the Continental Line. *Photo by Dr. Eric Nason, 2nd South Carolina Regiment.*

Dark blue leggings, of the same kind worn by ranger and rifle units of the American military forces. *Photo by Dr. Eric Nason, 2ⁿᵈ South Carolina Regiment.*

Black shoes, of the standard type worn by most of the Continental foot units. *Photo by Dr. Eric Nason, 2ⁿᵈ South Carolina Regiment.*

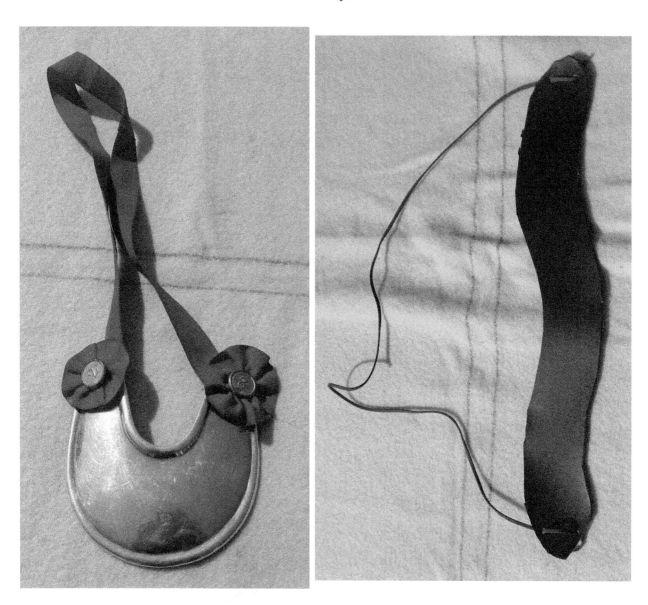

(Left) White metal gorget, of the standard type worn by officers and by several NCOs of the Continental Army. The gorget was a symbol of rank and the last surviving element of the cuirasses worn during the XVII century. *Photo by Dr. Eric Nason, 2nd South Carolina Regiment.*

(Right) Some small pieces of leather, like the one reproduced here, were worn under the collar by many of the Continental infantrymen for protection of the neck against enemy swords and bayonets. The Continental Marines also used these as protection against sword cuts, giving rise to their nickname of "leathernecks". *Photo by Dr. Eric Nason, 2nd South Carolina Regiment.*

Red knapsack used by the Continental infantry. Sometimes the regimental number could be embroidered on the back. *Photo by Dr. Eric Nason, 2nd South Carolina Regiment.*

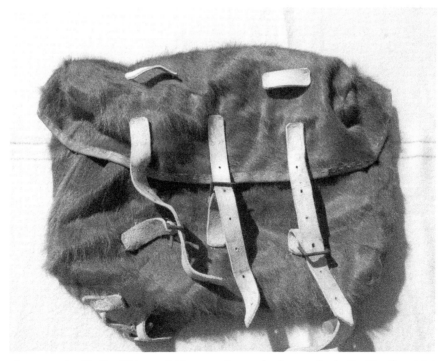

French knapsack, covered with fur. This model became increasingly popular in the Continental Army after France became an ally of the USA. *Photo by Dr. Eric Nason, 2nd South Carolina Regiment.*

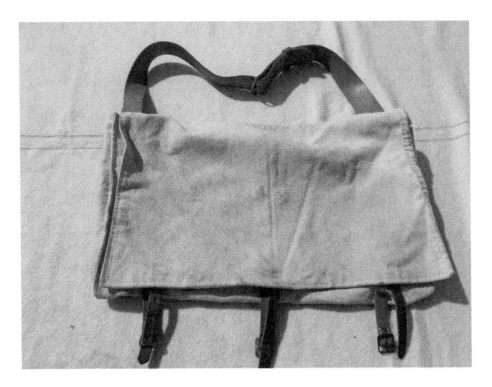

White canvas knapsack, of the model used by most of the Continental infantrymen. *Photo by Dr. Eric Nason, 2nd South Carolina Regiment.*

White canvas haversack, of the standard model employed by the great majority of the Continentals. *Photo by Dr. Eric Nason, 2nd South Carolina Regiment.*

Metal canteen, made of tin with a cork stopper. *Photo by Dr. Eric Nason, 2nd South Carolina Regiment.*

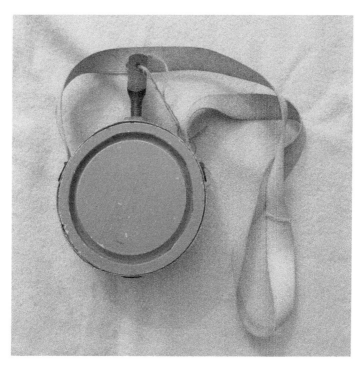

Wooden canteen, painted in light blue. *Photo by Dr. Eric Nason, 2nd South Carolina Regiment.*

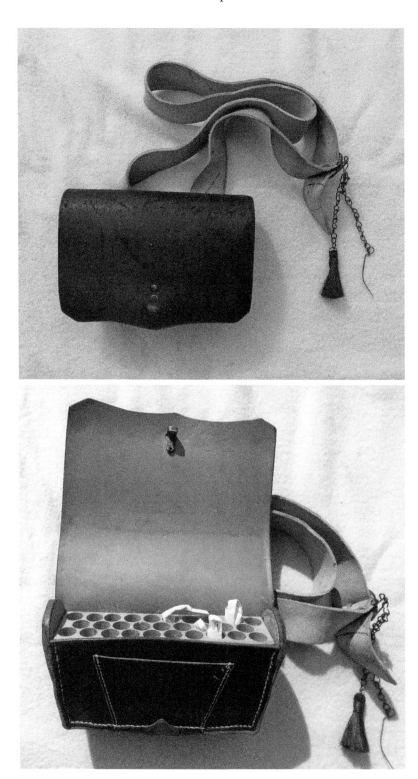

A black leather cartridge box, of the standard model used by the Continental infantry including a detail of the wooden block drilled out to hold 36 cartridges. To the left is a brush and pick used to clean out the pan and to touch the hole. Photo by Dr. Eric Nason, 2nd South Carolina Regiment.

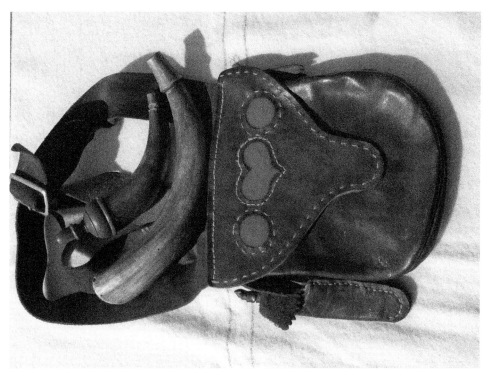

(Top) Brown leather bag and horns for the black powder, used by the riflemen of the Continental Army. *Photo by Dr. Eric Nason, 2nd South Carolina Regiment.*

(Bottom) Each Continental infantryman carried some accessories inside his knapsack; these included a folding knife, a bag of flints, some spare flints, a spring vice and some musket tools (a knapping hammer, a vent pick, a pan brush and a screwdriver). *Photo by Dr. Eric Nason, 2nd South Carolina Regiment.*

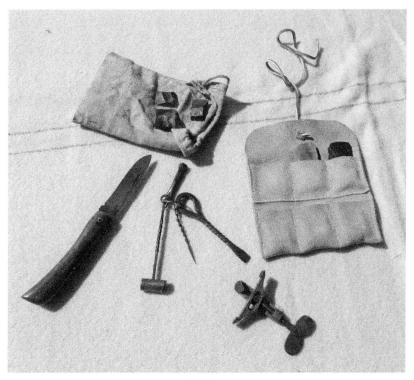

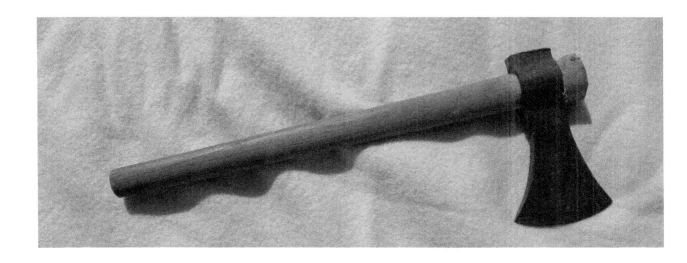

Hatchets were used by most of the Continental foot soldiers - often as working tools but also, as a weapon for hand-to-hand fighting. *Photo by Dr. Eric Nason, 2nd South Carolina Regiment.*

Fascine knives such as the above were used around camps to cut brush and wood. In a pinch they were also used for protection.

When available, bayonets like the Brown Bess (above) and the Charleville (below) were triangular in shape and locked onto the musket.

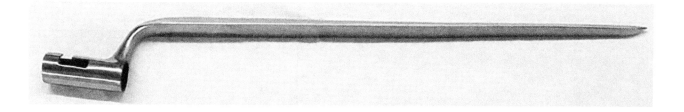

Detail of the mechanism of a flintlock musket. There is a guard on the
to keep it from accidentally firing. *Photo by the 1ˢᵗ Virginia Regiment of the Continental Line.*

"Kentucky" rifled musket, of the type used by most of the American ranger and rifle units. This was commonly a .40 - .48 calibre bullet. *Photo by Dr. Eric Nason, 2ⁿᵈ South Carolina Regiment.*

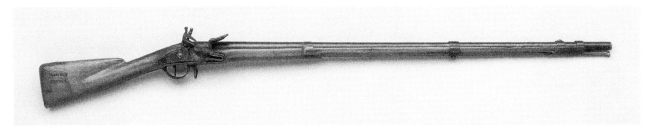

Model 1766 Infantry Musket. Probably made at Charleville Armory. This .69 calibre musket was used until the 1840's. Charleville, France. (*Museum of the American Revolution 2014.03.0001*).

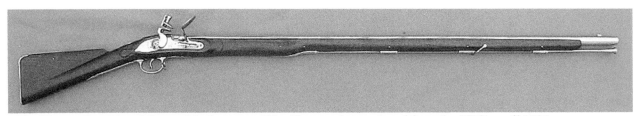

The "Brown Bess" Land Pattern Musket was a .75 calibre musket produced from the 1720's until 1838.

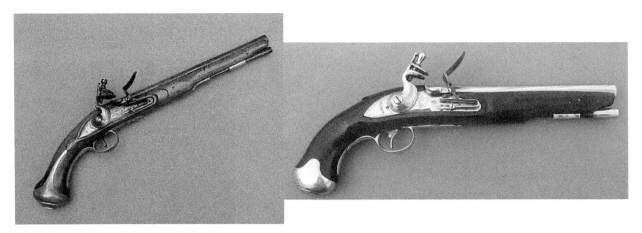

(Left) Heavy dragoon pistol developed in the 1730's; it fired a .62 calibre ball but was not accurate at more than a dozen yards. The light dragoon pistol (right), also firing a .62 calibre bullet, was produced in the 1760's and replaced the heavy dragoon pistol for cavalry operations in North America.

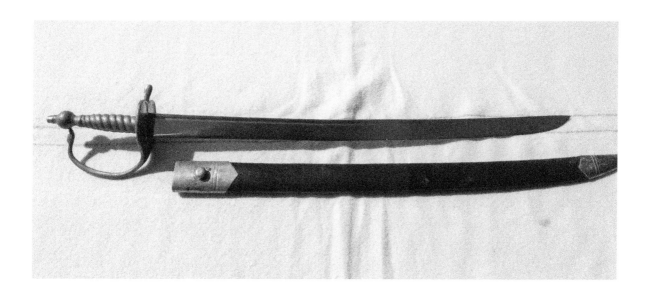

Sword of a line infantry officer. Officers and some NCOs had swords as side-arms and used these to keep their men in line. *Photo by Dr. Eric Nason, 2nd South Carolina Regiment.*

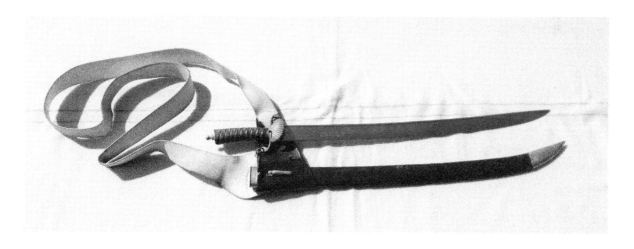

Sword of a line infantry NCO. *Photo by Dr. Eric Nason, 2nd South Carolina Regiment.*

This military drum dates to 1740 and was made by Robert Crosman of Taunton (Massachusetts). Museum of the American Revolution 2003.00.0897-2003.00.0898.

George Washington's campaign tent. Museum of the American Revolution

Select bibliography

René Chartrand, *Canadian Military Heritage: Volume II (1755-1871)*, Art Global, 1995

René Chartrand, *Colonial American Troops 1610-1774 (1)*, Osprey Publishing, 2002

René Chartrand, *Colonial American Troops 1610-1774 (2)*, Osprey Publishing, 2003

René Chartrand, *Colonial American Troops 1610-1774 (3)*, Osprey Publishing, 2003

René Chartrand, *American War of Independence Commanders*, Osprey Publishing, 2003

René Chartrand, *American Loyalist Troops 1775-1784*, Osprey Publishing, 2008

Fred Funcken and Liliane Funcken, *L'uniforme et les Armes des Soldats des Etats-Unis: L'infanterie et la marine*, Casterman, 1979

Fred Funcken and Liliane Funcken, *L'uniforme et les Armes des Soldats des Etats-Unis: La cavallerie et l'artillerie*, Casterman, 1979

Ed Gilbert and Catherine Gilbert, *Patriot Militiaman in the American Revolution 1775-1782*, Osprey Publishing, 2015

Michael G. Johnson, *American Woodland Indians*, Osprey Publishing, 1990

Philip Katcher, *The American Provincial Corps 1775-1784*, Osprey Publishing, 1973

Daniel Marston, *The American Revolution 1774-1783*, Osprey Publishing, 2002

John Milsop, *Continental infantryman of the American Revolution*, Osprey Publishing, 2004

John Mollo, *Uniforms of the American Revolution in colour*, Blandford Press, 1975

Digby Smith and Kevin F. Riley, *An illustrated encyclopedia of uniforms from 1775-1783: the American Revolutionary War*, Lorenz Books, 2008

The Company of Military Historians, *Military uniforms in America: the Era of the American Revolution*, Presidio Press, 1975

Russell F. Weigley, *History of the United States Army*, Macmillan Press, 1967

Martin Windrow, *Military Dress of North America 1665-1970*, Charles Scribner's Sons, 1973

Peter Young, *George Washington's Army*, Osprey Publishing, 1972

Gary Zaboly, *American Colonial Ranger*, Osprey Publishing, 2004

Marko Zlatich, *General Washington's Army 1: 1775-1778*, Osprey Publishing, 1994

Marko Zlatich, *General Washington's Army 2: 1779-1783*, Osprey Publishing, 1995

INDEX

About the author

Gabriele Esposito is a military historian who works as a freelance author and researcher for some of the most important publishing houses in the military history sector. In particular, he is an expert specializing in uniformology: his interests and expertise range from the ancient civilizations to modern post-colonial conflicts. During recent years he has conducted and published several works on the military history of the Latin American countries, with special attention on the War of the Triple Alliance and the War of the Pacific. He is among the leading experts on the military history of the Italian Wars of Unification and the Spanish Carlist Wars. His books and essays are published on a regular basis by Osprey Publishing, Pen & Sword, Winged Hussar Publishing and Libreria Editrice Goriziana; he is also the author of numerous military history articles appearing in specialized magazines like *Ancient Warfare Magazine*, *Medieval Warfare Magazine*, *The Armourer*, *History of War*, *Guerres et Histoire*, *Focus Storia* and *Focus Storia Wars*.

The reenactors who contributed to this book

The **2nd Regiment, South Carolina Continental Line** is a living history organization first formed in 1975. The unit is a volunteer living history organization dedicated to recreating the daily activities and experiences of one of the most famous American units of the Revolutionary War. Our group of men, women and children desire to bring the era of our nation's birth to life through battle re-enactments and living history demonstrations. The 2nd SC Regiment is also a member of the Continental Line, an association of American Revolutionary War units along the east coast. We can be followed on www.2ndsc.org and on Facebook.

The **1st Virginia Regiment of the Continental Line** is a recreated Revolutionary War living history group. The organization is composed of volunteers who authentically clothe and equip themselves to portray the soldiers and families of this historic military unit. The original 1st Virginia Regiment was, of course, a part of the Continental Army under the command of His Excellency Gen. George Washington. The recreated First Virginia Regiment is one of the most recognized Revolutionary War units in the country and has itself developed a proud history. Organized in February 1975, the First Virginia is incorporated in Virginia as a non-profit, educational organization. For additional information on the First Virginia Regiment please visit our website www.1varegiment.com and our Facebook page.

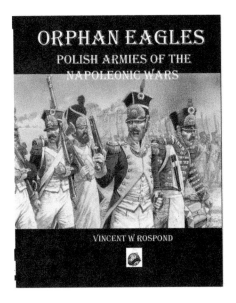

Look for more books from Winged Hussar Publishing, LLC – E-books, paperbacks and Limited Edition hardcovers. The best in history, science fiction and fantasy at:

https://www. wingedhussarpublishing.com
or follow us on Facebook at:
Winged Hussar Publishing LLC
Or on twitter at:
WingHusPubLLC

For information and upcoming publications

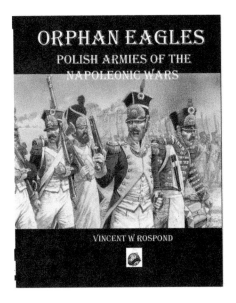

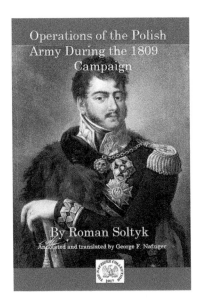

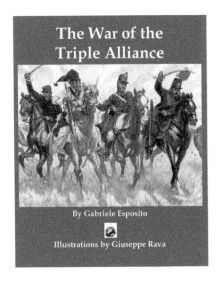

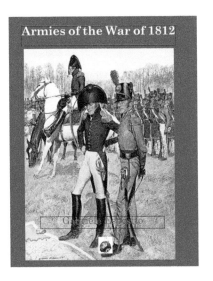

Gabriele Esposito

Printed in the United States